Jacqueline Wilson
Secrets
Illustrated by Nick Sharratt

Jacqueline Wilson
LIZZIE ZIPMOUTH
Illustrated by Nick Sharratt

CORGI PUPS
Perfect for new readers
THE Monster Story-Teller
Jacqueline Wilson
Illustrated by Nick Sharratt

Jacqueline Wilson
Tracy Beaker
Illustrated by Nick Sharratt
KU-021-782

JACQUELINE WILSON
THE STORY OF HER CHILDHOOD
Jacky Daydream
Illustrated by Nick Sharratt

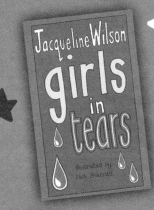
Jacqueline Wilson
girls in tears
Illustrated by Nick Sharratt

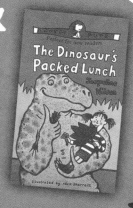
CORGI PUPS
Perfect for new readers
The Dinosaur's Packed Lunch
Jacqueline Wilson
Illustrated by Nick Sharratt

Jacqueline Wilson
Vicky Angel
Illustrated by Nick Sharratt

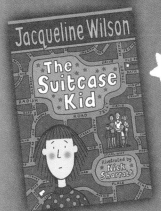
Jacqueline Wilson
The Suitcase Kid
Illustrated by Nick Sharratt

Jacqueline Wilson
THE CAT MUMMY
Illustrated by Nick Sharratt

Jacqueline Wilson
BAD GIRLS
Illustrated by Nick Sharratt

Jacqueline Wilson
The Illustrated Mum
Illustrated by Nick Sharratt

Jacqueline Wilson
The WORRY Website
Illustrated by Nick Sharratt

Jacqueline Wilson
Dustbin Baby
Illustrated by Nick Sharratt

Jacqueline Wilson
girls out late
Illustrated by Nick Sharratt

JACQUELINE WILSON
CHILDREN'S LAUREATE 2005-2007
CANDYFLOSS
NICK SHARRATT

Totally Jacqueline Wilson

Totally Jacqueline Wilson

The Essential Jacqueline Wilson Experience!

Illustrated by Nick Sharratt

Doubleday

TOTALLY JACQUELINE WILSON
A DOUBLEDAY BOOK 978 0 385 61252 4

Published in Great Britain by Doubleday,
an imprint of Random House Children's Books
A Random House Group Company

This edition published 2007

1 3 5 7 9 10 8 6 4 2

Text copyright © Jacqueline Wilson, 2007
Illustrations copyright © Nick Sharratt, 2007
Illustrations pp 14, 15 copyright © Sue Heap, 1995

Book covers on pp58-59 reprinted with kind permission of the publishers.

'The Real Rebecca' originally published in 2003 in *Kids' Night In* (HarperCollins)
'Problems' originally published in 2002 in *BBC Children in Need Collection*
'Odd One Out' originally published in 2003 in *Eating Candyfloss Upside Down* (Puffin)
'Hunt the Baby' originally published in the *Young Telegraph*
My Mum and Dad Make Me Laugh by Nick Sharratt shown on p68
Cover illustration © 1994 Nick Sharratt
Reproduced by permission of Walker Books Ltd, London SE11 5HJ

RANDOM HOUSE CHILDREN'S BOOKS
61–63 Uxbridge Road, London W5 5SA
www.kidsatrandomhouse.co.uk

THE RANDOM HOUSE GROUP Limited Reg. No. 954009
Addresses for companies within the Random House Group Limited
can be found at: www.randomhouse.co.uk

A CIP catalogue record for this book is available from the British Library.

Designed by Clair Stutton
Compiled by Alex Antscherl

Printed and bound in Singapore

For
Anna Rickards, with love

One day I might write the
story of Cynthia B. Sunshade!

Jacqueline Wilson

xxx

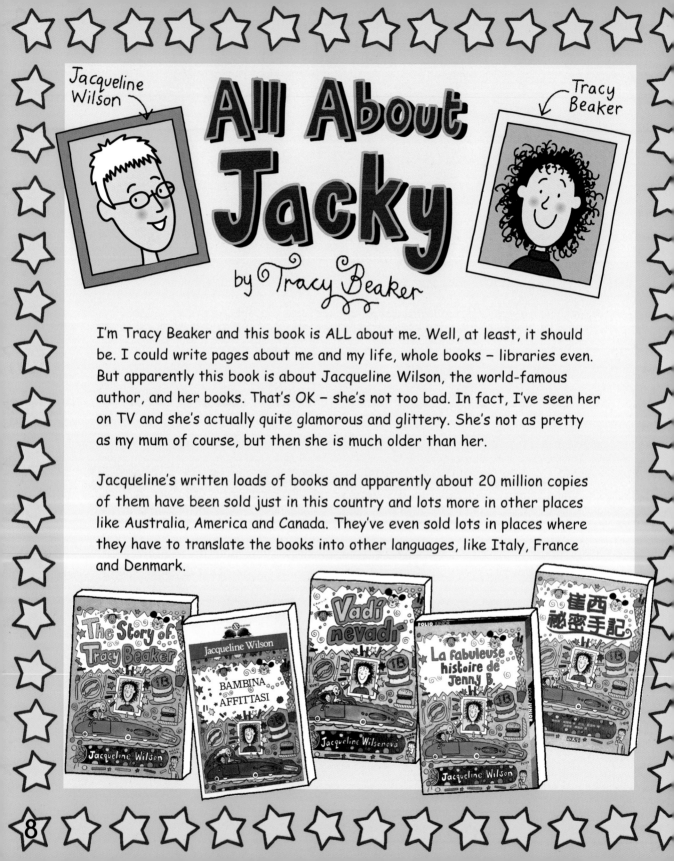

Jacqueline Wilson

Tracy Beaker

All About Jacky

by Tracy Beaker

I'm Tracy Beaker and this book is ALL about me. Well, at least, it should be. I could write pages about me and my life, whole books – libraries even. But apparently this book is about Jacqueline Wilson, the world-famous author, and her books. That's OK – she's not too bad. In fact, I've seen her on TV and she's actually quite glamorous and glittery. She's not as pretty as my mum of course, but then she is much older than her.

Jacqueline's written loads of books and apparently about 20 million copies of them have been sold just in this country and lots more in other places like Australia, America and Canada. They've even sold lots in places where they have to translate the books into other languages, like Italy, France and Denmark.

Jacqueline's been writing books for years – since she was nine years old, much younger than I am. When she was first grown-up she worked as a journalist and the company she worked for even named a magazine after her. Cam Lawson, my friend who's a writer (although a lot less gorgeous and rich than lucky old Jacqueline), says she used to read *Jackie* magazine when she was young.

Of course, when I'm grown-up I'll be a famous writer too and people will probably be saying, 'Jacqueline Wilson? Never heard of her. We love Tracy Beaker's books.' But I have to admit Jacqueline's pretty popular right now. She's won loads of prizes, like the Guardian Fiction Award (that's one from a proper grown-up newspaper) and the Smarties Prize. I know which one I'd rather win. I mean, who wouldn't rather have a bucketload of chocolate instead of some boring little statue to put on your mantelpiece? Jacqueline's even been given an award by the Queen – an OBE. Elaine the Pain (my very annoying social worker) said I'd probably be an OBE when I grow up, which I thought was pretty cool. Until she told me it would stand for 'Orrible Big 'Ead in my case.

Jacky FACT

Jacqueline has a full-size rocking horse in her house

Jacqueline has been the Children's Laureate, which is a way of saying that she's one of the most important children's authors in the country. So I suppose it is sort of fair that this book is mostly about her. There'll be loads of books about me when I'm famous too.

The TOP FIFTY Questions

BATH

KINGSTON

WHERE WERE YOU BORN?

Bath, Somerset, but I've lived in Kingston in Surrey since I was three.

HOW OLD ARE YOU?

Older than your mum but maybe not as old as your granny.

WHAT'S YOUR FAVOURITE FILM?

An old black-and-white movie called *Mandy* about a little girl who couldn't hear.

WHAT SORT OF FAMILY DO YOU HAVE?

I have one lovely grown-up daughter, Emma (and a fiercely independent old mum who lives ten minutes away). I don't have any brothers or sisters, though I have always longed to be part of a big family.

DO YOU HAVE ANY PETS?

I am a foster mother to my friend's very pretty but very fat tortoiseshell cat, Whisky. I still want a little black poodle some day.

WHAT'S YOUR FAVOURITE FOOD?

I like fruit most. I also like cakes and chips and ice cream (but not all together).

WHAT SORT OF HOUSE DO YOU LIVE IN?

I used to live in a tiny terraced house but now I live in a beautiful Victorian house with lots more space for all my books. My life-sized fashion model Crystal now shares my splendid dressing room, and all my dolls and teddies and monkeys have new corners to crouch in.

WHAT ARE YOUR HOBBIES?

I like reading, going to art galleries and films, swimming (50 lengths in my local pool before breakfast every morning).

WHEN IS YOUR BIRTHDAY?

17 December, which is a pity as it's so near Christmas.

WHAT DO YOU LOOK LIKE?

I'm small and skinny with very short spiky hair and silver glasses. I nearly always wear black and I have a big ring on every finger.

You've Always Wanted to Ask Jacqueline

WHAT'S YOUR FAVOURITE TV PROGRAMME?
I don't watch television often, but I always watch *ER*. My favourite children's TV show has to be *The Story of Tracy Beaker*! (Tracy would beat me up if I said otherwise!)

24 WHICH IS YOUR FAVOURITE OUT OF ALL YOUR BOOKS?
I can never make up my mind. Maybe *The Illustrated Mum*.

25 WHICH BOOK HAS WON THE MOST AWARDS?
I think it's probably *Double Act*. It won the Smarties Prize, the Children's Book of the Year Award and the Sheffield Book of the Year.

23 HOW MANY BOOKS HAVE YOU PUBLISHED?
About 90? I've lost count!

12 WHAT SORT OF MUSIC DO YOU LIKE?
All sorts - especially Queen and the late lamented Freddie Mercury.

22 WERE YOU EVER MARRIED?
I was married to a man called Millar, but we're divorced now.

21 WHO WAS YOUR FIRST BOYFRIEND?
He was called Alan and he had fair hair. He wrote me my first love letter.

20 WHO WAS YOUR BEST FRIEND AT SCHOOL?
A girl called Chris. We're still friends.

13 WHAT'S YOUR FAVOURITE COLOUR?
Black and silver.

14 WHAT'S YOUR FAVOURITE ANIMAL?
A lemur.

17 WHICH SCHOOL DID YOU GO TO?
Latchmere Primary School and Coombe Girls Secondary School.

19 DID YOU ALWAYS WANT TO BE A WRITER?
Yes, from the age of six I was always making up stories.

WHAT WAS YOUR FAVOURITE SUBJECT AT SCHOOL?
I liked English and art.

15 WHAT WAS YOUR WORST SUBJECT AT SCHOOL?
I hated maths and I was useless at PE.

18 DID YOU HAVE ANY JOB APART FROM WRITING?
I was a journalist in my late teens. The girls' magazine *Jackie* was named after me!

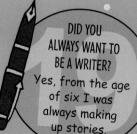

HAVE ANY OF YOUR BOOKS BEEN MADE INTO A TV SERIES?

There have been five series of *Tracy Beaker*, plus one spin-off film. *Double Act, The Illustrated Mum, Best Friends* and *Girls in Love* have all had excellent television adaptations.

HAVE YOU EVER WRITTEN FOR ADULTS?

I've written five crime novels – but they all had children in them.

WHY DO YOU ALWAYS WRITE ABOUT GIRLS?

I do sometimes write about boys. *Cliffhanger* and *Buried Alive!* are about Tim and his best friend Biscuits.

DO YOU KNOW ANY OTHER CHILDREN'S WRITERS?

Heaps! Some are my special friends.

HAVE ANY OF YOUR BOOKS BEEN STAGED?

Vicky Ireland has adapted and directed *The Lottie Project, Double Act, Bad Girls* and *Midnight*! Mary Morris has written a stage play, *Tracy Beaker Gets Real*.

WHERE DO YOU GET YOUR IDEAS FROM?

I don't know. They just seem to pop into my head.

WHAT ARE YOUR FAVOURITE BOOKS NOW?

I love *Jane Eyre* by Charlotte Bronte, *The Bell Jar* by Sylvia Plath and Katherine Mansfield's short stories. My favourite children's picture book now is *Where the Wild Things Are* by Maurice Sendak.

WHICH WAS YOUR FAVOURITE BOOK WHEN YOU WERE A CHILD?

I loved an American book called *Nancy and Plum* by Betty MacDonald about two sisters who run away from an orphanage. I also liked Noel Streatfeild's stories (especially *Ballet Shoes*) and *Little Women* and *What Katy Did*.

WHO IS YOUR FAVOURITE CHARACTER IN YOUR BOOKS?

I'm very fond of Tracy Beaker even though she's totally outrageous.

WHY ARE THERE TWO ILLUSTRATORS FOR DOUBLE ACT?

Because Ruby and Garnet are meant to have done the pictures themselves. Nick drew all the Ruby illustrations and Nick's friend, Sue Heap, drew Garnet. They both look great. It's hard telling them apart.

DO YOU BASE YOUR CHARACTERS ON REAL PEOPLE?

No, it's much more fun making them all up. I wish some of them were real though. I'd love to meet Elsa from *The Bed and Breakfast Star* – she's such a kind, cheerful girl.

ARE YOUR BOOKS ALWAYS ILLUSTRATED BY NICK SHARRATT?

Nearly always. I absolutely love Nick's pictures. I'm very pleased and proud that we work together.

39 DO YOU EVER WRITE ABOUT TEENAGERS?
I've written four books about girls in Year Nine: *Girls in Love, Girls Under Pressure, Girls Out Late* and *Girls in Tears*. *Kiss* is also a teenage book – and so is *Love Lessons*.

40 IF YOU COULD HAVE ONE WISH FOR THE 21ST CENTURY WHAT WOULD IT BE?
That people still make up stories.

50 WHAT'S IT LIKE BEING A RICH AND FAMOUS WRITER?
It's wonderful – but it's hard work too.

48 HAVE YOU GOT ANY SPECIAL AMBITIONS?
I'd like to write 100 books. I'd also like to have a little spare time!

www.jacquelinewilson.co.uk

38 DO YOU HAVE A FAN CLUB?
Yes! It's on the website www.jacquelinewilson.co.uk and anyone can join. I write a special newsletter every month and there are all sorts of offers, jokes and information.

49 WHAT'S YOUR PROUDEST MOMENT?
Holding my new baby daughter in my arms.

46 WHAT'S BEEN YOUR MOST EMBARRASSING MOMENT?
Falling flat on my face at my first dance!

45 WHERE DO YOU WRITE?
I write in special pretty notebooks. I take one everywhere I go. I often write on trains! When my story is finished I type it out on my computer, changing bits and pieces as I go.

41 WHAT DID IT FEEL LIKE TO SEE YOUR FIRST BOOK IN THE SHOPS?
It felt absolutely fantastic.

47 DO YOU GET LOTS OF LETTERS AND E-MAILS FROM FANS?
I get lots of e-mails sent to the fan club. I can only reply to a few each month – I wish I could manage more! I also get around 200 letters a week. I read them all and try hard to write back to anyone who has sent a very special letter or a beautiful drawing. I also always write to any child who is ill or very worried about something. I wish I could clone myself so I could write to everyone.

42 DO YOU MEET LOTS OF CHILDREN?
I meet lots and lots of children. I talk at many literary festivals and libraries and I do big book signing tours twice a year. Sometimes people queue for five or six hours to get a book signed!

43 HOW LONG DOES IT TAKE YOU TO WRITE A BOOK?
Between three and six months.

44 DO YOU TRAVEL ALL OVER THE COUNTRY?
Yes, I zoom up and down Great Britain. I've even been lucky enough to do book tours in Australia and New Zealand too.

AUSTRALIA

An Interview with
Nick Sharratt

By Ruby and Garnet

Ruby → Hello, Mr Sharratt. How long have you been an illustrator?

Nick → Please, call me Nick. I've been a full-time illustrator ever since I finished art school, which was over twenty years ago.

Garnet → Wow! You must be really old now.

Ruby! Shhh! You can't say things like that.

Sorry, Nick. I know you're not old, not like Gran, not even like our dad. So, where did you go to art school?

First of all I did a foundation course in Manchester and then I went to London and studied at the St Martin's School of Art.

Did you always know you wanted to be an illustrator?

Even at primary school I was sure that I wanted to do something that involved art, and once I discovered illustration and graphic design I knew I'd found the perfect work for me.

Yes, I think that if you're born being really good at something you know you could do it for a living, don't you? It's like me and acting. It's just a shame Garnet got all nervous and silly at that audition we went to, otherwise we'd probably be famous actresses on telly by now.

Speak for yourself, Ruby. On second thoughts, it might be better if you spoke a bit less. We're supposed to be finding out about Nick Sharratt and all his pictures that are in Jacqueline Wilson's books.

Is that all you do, Nick? Just draw the pictures for Jacqueline's books?

With two new novels a year needing covers and inside artwork, plus the Jacqueline Wilson Diary and various other extra Jacky books, that keeps me busy, but no, I do lots of other work as well. Some of the things are connected with my work on Jacky's books. For example, I help with the animations for the *Tracy Beaker* TV series and check how my artwork is being used on merchandise such as Jacqueline Wilson pencil cases and so on. But I also illustrate picture books for

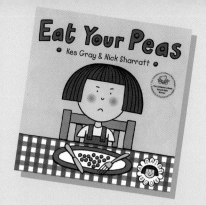

younger children, such as the hilarious stories about Daisy by Kes Gray and Pants by Giles Andreae. I also write and illustrate my own picture books, like *Shark in the Park*, *Ketchup on Your Cornflakes* and *Don't Put Your Finger in the Jelly, Nelly*.

Have you been working with Jacqueline for a long time?

Yes, actually, for more than fifteen years now. The first book of hers that I illustrated was *The Story of Tracy Beaker*, which was published in 1991, and there have been another 33 novels since then.

Gosh, don't you ever get fed up with each other?

No, we're good friends and always enjoy getting together when we have the chance.

Oh, I thought you probably lived in the same house . . .

Don't be silly, Ruby . . .

Actually, no, but lots of people think that. I live in Brighton on the south coast and Jacky lives in Kingston, in Surrey.

Do you work at home?

Yes, I have a studio at the top of my house. The seagulls peer through the window and watch me at my desk.

Do you work on one book at a time?

No, I have lots of projects on the go at the same time and I hardly ever spend the whole day working on just one book. I use the mornings for 'thinking' work: coming up with ideas and doing rough sketches. In the afternoon I usually do final artwork. I draw my black and white pictures in soft pencil or with a technical pen. I used to use charcoal and watercolour inks but now I do nearly all my colouring on my computer.

So are you stuck in your studio every day?

No, not every single day. I often have to go to London for meetings with publishers. I also sometimes do events for children at literary festivals and I've visited lots of schools over the years.

You're so busy. Do you ever get any time off?

Not much!

Do you ever get to have a holiday?

Yes, I have two or three lovely holidays a year and when I'm on holiday I don't do any drawing at all!

We were wondering where you get your ideas from? How do you decide what characters should look like?

Do you just stick to what Jacqueline says in the story?

I read the story very carefully and by the time I've finished it I've picked up enough clues to imagine how the author sees the characters. If you want to know more about how I create a character, and a cover for the book, why don't you turn to page 87?

Thanks, Nick, we will. It's been great talking to you.

Yeah, thanks very much. Perhaps we'll have a go at illustrating our story in our Accounts book now.

The Real Rebecca

A story by Jacqueline Wilson

101 Newton Street, Kingtown

Dear Jenna Williams

I know you probably get hundreds of letters every week. My little sister Molly has written to you in the past. It was the letter with all the glitter (left over from when she made her own Christmas cards) and it said in bright pink gel pen: DEAR JENA I AM YOUR NUMBER ONE FAN AND YOU ARE MY FAVORIT WRITER LOTS OF LOVE AND KISSES FROM MOLLY.

It's probably not the most eloquent letter you've ever received but she's only seven and it took her ages. I'm Molly's big brother, Jake. I don't want to sound rude but I'm afraid I'm not your number one fan. I haven't actually read many of your books. Especially not the lovey-dovey girly ones. We did read one in Year Five at primary school, the one about the really bad kid who runs away, and did you write that book about the boy who gets ill? If so, I've read that one too. But I'm not really into that sort of real-life stuff, especially not now I'm thirteen.

I like fantasy. I don't just read it, I write it too. I've made up this entire world, Jakarabia, and I live there, and there are various tribes who live in different parts, the Junglies and the Seaswimmers and the Mountain-Hoppers, and I'm the leader of all of them, and then there are all these different weird animals and some alien creatures too – well, I won't go on about it, you don't want to listen to all my stupid story, though actually I tell it to Molly sometimes when she can't sleep at night and she seems to love it. But I think she actually likes your books a bit more. She's got this whole shelf-full and she reads them over and over and colours in all the pictures with her gel pens and sticks gold and silver stars all over the covers.

Jakarabian Wildlife

So when Mum saw you were coming to Kingtown last Saturday to do a book-signing she thought Molly might like to come and meet you.

'Meet Jenna Williams?' said Molly, like you were the Queen and David Beckham and Britney Spears all rolled into one person. 'Oh yes please yes please yes please!' I don't get why she got so excited. I mean, no offence, but you don't have a crown and a palace and you don't play football and you can't sing, you're just an ordinary old lady who writes kids' books.

But Molly likes your books, and she got so worked up on Friday night she couldn't get to sleep for ages and I had to tell her Jakarabia stories until I was hoarse. In fact, I invented an entirely new tribe of Cavedwellers who tell stories all night long and they start off in great booming voices and finish at dawn in hoarse whispers.

None left.

I was still a bit croaky at breakfast on Saturday morning so I gulped down a little milk to soothe my throat. And a bowl or two of cornflakes to go with it. Mum got a bit narked with me because there wasn't quite enough milk or cornflakes left and she and Molly had to make do with toast and juice.

'You're a hopeless greedy gannet, Jake,' she said crossly. 'I'll have to go shopping now and yet it's not pay day till next week.'

We haven't got that much cash. My dad doesn't always send the maintenance money for us when he should. Mum did have a boyfriend for a bit but it didn't work out. Basically, Molly and I couldn't stick him. So now we're back to Mum and Molly and me and we're fine. We're definitely not like one of those dysfunctional families in your books. No offence again, but why do you always write about people with problems????

Ex-boyfriend

Ugh!

Anyway, we had a slight problem Saturday morning. I wanted to spend my Saturday slobbing on the sofa, watching telly and maybe writing further chronicles of Jakarabia. But Mum wanted to go shopping and Molly wanted to meet Jenna Williams – you!

'I think there might be a bit of a queue at the bookshop,' said Mum. 'You come with us, Jake. Then you can stand in the queue with Molly while I go and do the shopping. It'll be much quicker that way. And I don't like leaving you in the house by yourself.'

'Mum! I'm not an infant. I'm a teenager,' I said, sighing heavily.

'Only just.' Mum came over to me and stood with her hands on her hips, looking down on me. Which is not hard to do. My mum's quite tall. And just at the moment, before my hormones kick in or whatever, I happen to be a tad on the short side. I'm sure any day now I'll shoot up rapidly to at least six foot. It's not for lack of nourishment, as Mum would rapidly agree.

'When you get bigger than me maybe I'll do what you say. Up till then, I'm the boss, OK?' said Mum. 'And I say you're coming into town with us, pal.'

'All right. If I must. But I don't want to stand in a queue with a whole lot of girls. I'll look like such a twit. You stand in the queue, Mum, and I'll do the shopping.'

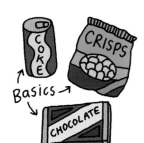

'Oh no. I don't trust you with my housekeeping purse! You'd forget the basics and just buy crisps and Coke and chocolate.'

'They're my basics.'

'Quite,' said Mum. 'No, I'll shop. You queue.'

'I hate queuing. It makes my legs ache,' I moaned.

'Well, we'll get there early, OK. It shouldn't be too long a queue,' said Mum.

Ha ha ha. The 'ha's represent mirthless sarcastic laughter.

We thought we were early. But the world and his wife and their small daughters must have been up at the crack of dawn because as soon as we got into Flowerfields shopping centre we saw this huge great queue snaking out of the first-floor bookshop, right down the stairs and way past the ornamental singing teddies.

'Oh my goodness,' said Mum.

'Oh total badness,' I said. 'This is crazy. We're going to be stuck here for hours and hours.'

'Maybe we won't bother,' said Mum. 'Molly, sweetheart, you won't mind terribly if we

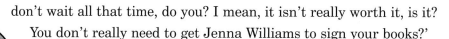

don't wait all that time, do you? I mean, it isn't really worth it, is it? You don't really need to get Jenna Williams to sign your books?'

We looked at Molly. She'd dressed up specially in her best pink T-shirt with the silver star and she'd smeared silver glitter gel all over her funny little face. She had all her dog-eared Jenna Williams collection crammed into a carrier bag. She was carrying it carefully as if it was the crown jewels. Her eyes blinked as Mum spoke. Her lip started quivering. A tear dripped down her glittery cheek. She didn't say anything. She didn't need to. Molly would mind *terribly* if we didn't wait. She *did* think it was worth it. She needed Jenna Williams to sign all her books.

I sighed. Mum sighed.

'OK,' said Mum. 'You join the back of the queue, Jake. I'll go and tackle the shopping. I'll try not to be too long.'

'Take your time,' I said. 'It looks as if Molly and I are going to be stuck here all morning. And afternoon. And most of the evening too.'

I took hold of Molly by her bony little elbow and steered her to the end of the queue,

Gorgeous!

behind a mum in jeans and high heels and a big sister with a tiny top and a little sister with a furry bag bulging with her Jenna Williams books.

Mum nodded at the other mum.

'I've got to go and do a bit of shopping. You'll keep an eye on them, won't you?' my mum said.

'Mum!' I hissed. Honestly, I felt so stupid. Mum was acting like I was a little kid. I glared at her. She grinned at me and rushed off. The other mum smiled at me too.

'More Jenna Williams fans?' she said.

'No, absolutely not,' I said quickly. 'I'm just here for my little sister. No, I can't stick Jenna Williams, actually.'

The big sister was looking at me.

And I was looking up at her.

She was GORGEOUS. Very slim, very tall, with a totally wonderfully fantastic figure. Her tight top looked truly astonishing. She was wearing tight jeans too, and little slip-on sandals that exposed her perfect pale feet, each nail polished pink.

Her Royal Highness, The Princess of Jakarabia

Girls with fantastic figures don't always have pretty faces. However, this girl wasn't just pretty, she was beautiful. Utterly beautiful, I tell you, with big blue eyes, tiny nose, rosebud mouth, heart-shaped face and a cloud of curly blonde hair down to her slender shoulders.

I think I am going to invent a Princess for Jakarabia. With blue eyes and curly hair. And a fantastic figure. She will of course be mine, because I rule over all Jakarabia, land and sea. So I will take the Princess as my royal consort and we will doubtless live happily ever after.

The girl in the queue was a total Princess. But she is not mine and this is not a fairy story so we aren't living happily ever after. Unless you act as our Fairy Godmother, Jenna Williams!!!

We got off to a bad start. I'd just said (please don't be hurt) that I didn't rate you or your books, right. This gorgeous girl looked at least fourteen so I was sure she'd be a bit old for them herself. I was convinced she was just in the queue to look after her little sister, like me. But I was wrong.

'I love Jenna Williams' books,' she said.

'Oh. Well. Of course I'm a boy,' I said. Then I blushed because that was such a daft thing to say. 'I mean, obviously I'm a boy, and well, Jenna Williams just writes for girls, doesn't she?'

'I don't think she sets out to write specifically for one sex or the other,' the girl said coolly.

I blushed again like a total nerd because she'd said the word sex. I hated myself for acting so stupidly. I'd have given everything to rewind my tape and start over. But this was real life, not the telly. She simply shook her head a little pityingly and turned her back on me. She had a cute little see-through plastic backpack, with three of Jenna Williams' teenage titles inside.

I wished I'd read the complete works of J.W. and could discuss them earnestly and intelligently. But I'd obviously blown it.

So I stayed there in the queue with Molly, wishing I was dead. Lots of people came and queued behind us. I soon couldn't see the end of the queue even when I craned my neck. I tried chatting to Molly to pass the time. I offered to tell her a new Jakarabia

instalment. I was desperate to show the girl in front that I was a cool, imaginative and caring kind of guy.

But Molly was feeling huffy with me because I'd stupidly said I didn't like boring old Jenna. Whoops! Sorry, no offence intended. You're not the slightest bit boring. I know. And only a little bit old.

'I'm fed up listening to your stories, Jake,' Molly said, sticking her nose in the air. 'I think I'll read one of my Jenna Williams books.'

'Ah. OK. Well, maybe I should give them a go too,' I said. I gave a little cough and raised my voice. 'It would be great if I could have a deck at one of her teenage titles, just to see what I've been missing.'

She must have heard me. I was practically bellowing into her ear. Well, I didn't quite reach up to her ear, but I'm speaking figuratively, right. Anyway, she didn't take a blind bit of notice. She just started nattering to her mum, ignoring me. And then her little sister started chatting to Molly, comparing notes on their favourite Jenna Williams books. I just stood there. Not talking to anyone. For hours.

Every quarter of an hour the ornamental clock chimed maddeningly and the teddy bear models started waving their paws and revolving their eyes. Then they started 'singing' in mad growly voices. I've never been very keen on that old song 'The Teddy Bears' Picnic'. But try having it growled again and again and again. You feel like going down to those woods and biffing them all in their big furry tummies.

I was not a happy guy.

Mum came back with her shopping. She'd got bars of chocolate and Coke for Molly and me. She gave some to the Princess and her little sister too. Little sister was called Hannah but for endless ages I didn't have a clue what big sister was called. I couldn't get up the nerve to ask her outright.

I know this might strike you as a bit odd because down on paper I am dead articulate. In fact, I tend to go on a bit too much. This is the sixth page of my letter and I still haven't got to the point. Well, we're nearly there.

When I was nearly in front of you I found out the Princess's name. You asked her, as you signed her teenage books. She smiled at you and said she was called Rebecca. Beautiful name. You signed her books and then you signed little Hannah's books and then it was Molly's turn. Only you might remember, our Molly suddenly went all white and whimpery and wouldn't budge. I couldn't believe it! Molly's never the least bit shy. And we'd waited in your wretched queue for hours and now it looked like she wasn't even going to say hello to you.

So I seized Molly by the wrist and pulled her up to your signing table and Molly hung her head and wouldn't look at you. But it was OK in the end because you started chatting to her, saying you loved her silver glitter and the silver star on her T-shirt and you let her try on one of your silver rings. Do you remember? Molly won't ever forget. You signed her books and she skipped all the way home, even though her legs must have been aching after all that queuing.

I trudged home. My legs were certainly aching. And my heart.

I had hoped to catch up with Rebecca and ask her out. But by the time Molly had cheered up and got all her books signed, Rebecca and Hannah and their mum had disappeared out of the shop.

I'd lost my chance. I had hours and hours when I could have asked her but I just couldn't get up the courage. I'm just a hopeless wimp.

So how about helping me out, Jenna Williams??? I know you've got your own website. Please can you tell my story and ask any stunningly beautiful, tall, teenage girl called Rebecca (with a sister called Hannah) who was in that ludicrously long queue at Kingtown to get in touch with me, as I care about her passionately and am desperate to see her again. Please please please!

In feverish anticipation

Jake Wilson

HAPHAZARD HOUSE   CHILDREN'S BOOKS

Dear Jake

Thank you so much for your letter. I enjoyed reading it enormously. I shall keep it carefully and then when you're a best-selling fantasy author I shall boast that I have a very special letter written by you.

If you look on my website you will see that I have indeed told your story – and if Rebecca writes then I will put you in touch with each other, so long as your mums give their permission. Fingers crossed! I love the idea of being a Fairy Godmother.

Give my love to Molly.

All good wishes

Jenna Williams

3 Feltham Drive
Kingtown

Dear Jenna Williams

This is so weird! I am a big fan of your books and so I very happily queued for ages and ages when you came to Kingtown the other week. Of course you won't remember me - but I was the one with fair curls exploding all over the place and a too-small T-shirt and my mum embarrassed me by telling you I wanted to be a writer too.

But you were ever so encouraging and you signed my books and you signed my little sister Hannah's books too.

I'm Rebecca - so this is why I'm writing to you!

I read all about this boy Jake on your website.

Don't tell him, but I don't even remember seeing him in the queue! I've been racking my brains and I can't think of any boy standing behind me. But he must have been there because he knows all about me! Admittedly his descriptions of me are exaggerated in the extreme. I am NOT NOT NOT a gorgeous Princess and my figure is certainly not fabulous. I'm not tall and slender, I'm small and a bit dumpy. But I don't mind a bit that Jake seems to think I look OK! Please put me in touch with him.

Love from Rebecca

101 Newton Street
Kingtown

Dear Jenna Williams

Oh woe!

She was the wrong Rebecca.

She was OK. I mean, she was actually quite good to talk to. Weirdly enough, I didn't feel a bit shy with her. I nattered on like anything. I even told her about Jakarabia and she seemed quite interested. She writes too. She actually came up with some relatively interesting ideas that might well get incorporated in future Jakarabia tales.

But it was all a bit pointless because she isn't the Princess of my dreams. She's just this ordinary bit-plumpish fair thirteen-year-old.

So where is the real Rebecca???? I will languish after my Princess for ever and a day. It is my fate.

Yours in despair

Jake Wilson

X X X X X X X

These aren't from me, they're from Molly.

Dear Jake

Oh woe too!

I had a feeling she might well be the wrong Rebecca. It's a very common name (though beautiful). Ditto Hannah. And she certainly didn't sound a vision of beauty. But do you know why I put you in touch with her? Because I couldn't help wondering if she might be the RIGHT Rebecca for you. You should meet up with her again!

I don't think it's a good idea to languish after the real Rebecca. I am not an Agony Aunt but I can't resist reminding you that Princesses can sometimes turn out to be frogs – even totally gorgeous ones with fabulous figures. And you thought she was at least fourteen, so she's technically an Older Woman. Maybe this bothers her. She didn't sound especially warm and friendly to you. There's another slightly delicate point. You mentioned she was tall. Perhaps it might be a little uncomfortable if she looked down on you, both figuratively and literally. Remember how irritating this is when your mum does it!

Perhaps Fate decreed that you and the other funny, friendly Rebecca were right for each other but it would have been too predictably boring to have a Boy meets Girl/Boy loses Girl/Boy finds Girl story. If I were writing your story I'd much prefer the twist of Boy meets Girl/Boy loses Girl/Boy doesn't find Girl/Boy finds another Girl.

What do you think?

All good wishes

Jenna Williams

XXXXXXXXXXXXXXXXXXXXXXXXXXXX for Molly

101 Newton Street, Kingtown
13 Feltham Drive, Kingtown

Dear Old Agony Auntie Jenna

   If your books stop selling some day maybe you could become a real Agony Aunt because you give really good advice!

   We are best friends now and we meet up nearly every day. We are writing a brand new story together. It's a fantasy story. We don't write real-life stuff. But you do. We wondered if you might like to write our story?

   Yours very happily indeed

     Jake and Rebecca

HAPHAZARD HOUSE CHILDREN'S BOOKS

Dear Jake and Rebecca
   Maybe I will write your story. And we'll get Molly to illustrate it with silver glitter hearts!
   With very very best wishes

     Jenna Williams

Mandy and Tanya from *Bad Girls*

So you think you know about

FRIENDSHIP

in Jacqueline Wilson's books?

Test yourself and all your friends to see who's the most clued up, then check your answers on page 128.

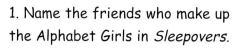

1. Name the friends who make up the Alphabet Girls in *Sleepovers*.

2. Who is the 'Bad Girl' who befriends Mandy White?

3. With which girl does Elsa become friends in *The Bed and Breakfast Star*?

4. And where does she meet her?

5. In *Secrets*, what does India call her diary 'friend'? (Do you know why?)

6. Who invites Biscuits to go on holiday with him in *Buried Alive*?

7. Who is Louise's new best friend in *The Story of Tracy Beaker*?

8. In *Candyfloss* when Floss has to go shopping with her friend Rhiannon, what does Rhiannon's mum buy them?

9. Name the two new friends Tracy Beaker makes in *The Dare Game*.

10. Which child types in a worry about friendship on *The Worry Website*?

11. What does Gemma take as a present when she goes to Scotland to visit her best friend Alice?

12. What's the name of the little boy that Charlie befriends when her mum babysits for him?

13. What club does Jade want her best friend Vicky to join at the beginning of *Vicky Angel*?

14. Why does Verity envy her friend Sophie in *The Cat Mummy*?

15. Who is the third boy in the Tigers team with Tim and Biscuits in *Cliffhanger*?

What's a Signing Event Really Like?

Hours and hours in a queue, clutching your brand-new book and several dog-eared old ones, your mum anxiously looking at her watch and your little brother whining, while with mounting excitement you creep gradually closer to the silver-haired lady sitting behind a table with a purple pen in her beringed fingers . . .

Sounds familiar? Well, you must have been to an event where Jacqueline Wilson was signing books. You know how it felt from your point of view – perhaps at once both thrilling (meeting Jacky) and tiring (waiting for hours), fun (making friends in the queue) and a little bit nerve-racking (deciding what to say to your favourite author). But have you ever thought about who else is involved and what it's like from their point of view?

Naomi

the publicist who organizes Jacqueline's events and tours

Long before a tour, I'll have received dozens of requests from bookshops for Jacky to come and sign copies of her new book. I have to work out how many visits Jacky can fit in during a two-week tour and whereabouts in the country we can reach. Sometimes we end up hurtling from one end of Britain to the next and back again in just a couple of days. I always ask the shops we're going to visit to bear in mind just how many people will come and how long they might have to wait. Jacqueline's famous for attracting hundreds of fans and the longest signing Jacky has ever done was eight hours non-stop. The shops have to make arrangements to fit all the fans in safely and, if possible, give them something to do while they're waiting . . .

Bob

the driver who chauffeurs Jacqueline to events

I often leave home at the crack of dawn to collect Jacqueline and get her to an event on time. When she is in the car we ask Tracy to trace the best route. Tracy is our navigation system named by Jacqueline after one of her characters – I wonder which one?!

Sometimes we go via the post office to pick up extra mail that the poor postman has been unable to carry on his round. Jacqueline sits in the back and tries to read and answer letters, and also writes the next book!

We know we have arrived at our destination when we see a huge queue of 400 or 500 fans blocking the street. Sometimes I go into the bookshop and help Naomi and the bookshop staff organize all of you in the queue.

After Jacqueline has signed the book of the last person in the queue, we head for home, exhausted but having had a wonderful time meeting you all.

Many of you will have noticed the similarities between a character in *Clean Break* and myself. I didn't know about this until, having spent a day with Jacqueline signing over 3,000 copies of *Clean Break* for shops we were unable to include in the tour, Jacqueline handed me a book and told me to read Chapter 13. Can you imagine my surprise and pleasure in seeing my name in it! I've even been asked to sign copies of it by some of you. COOL! So next time we meet at an event you can say you have met one of Jacqueline's characters. See you all soon.

Gary a bookseller

I have been very lucky as I have hosted four amazing signing sessions with Jacky over the years and I have to say that it is the best part of my job! When I found out that Jacky was coming to visit our shop in Worthing to sign copies of her book *Candyfloss* I started getting organized at once. The first thing I thought about was how to make the day lots of fun, to make sure that we could entertain all the fans while they were waiting to meet Jacky. As *Candyfloss* features a beautiful carousel, I managed to get one just the same outside the shop, and a candyfloss machine at the beginning of the very long queue.

On the day, I arrived at work very early to set up our bookshop for Jacky's event and there were already two fans waiting by the door. I put out a table and chair in the children's section of the shop and covered the table in bright pink fabric to match the cover of *Candyfloss* and then I displayed hundreds of copies of Jacky's books for the fans to buy and get signed. Jacky arrived and was so excited by the carousel that she had her picture taken on it. I made Jacky a cup of coffee and put out some chocolate biscuits (she has a sweet tooth). Meanwhile Naomi and I kept an eye on the queue of fans already forming. The bookshop staff spent the day looking after everyone in the queue, handing out Jacqueline Wilson activity sheets and sweets, and also making sure that the fans had their books open, ready to be signed. Then, bang on time, Jacqueline nipped behind the signing desk and looked up with a big smile ready to meet all her fans.

The best part of the day for me was meeting all the fans. They're bursting with questions to ask Jacky and are so excited but, as soon as they come face to face with their idol, BANG! – they go quiet, absolutely star-struck.

Many hours later, after Jacky finally reached the very last fan patiently waiting, there was just time for Jacky, me, Naomi and my manager to have a quick go on the carousel.

If Jacky ever visits a bookshop near you, go along and meet her as she is so lovely and would love to meet you . . .

Jade
a huge Jacky fan

When I heard that Jacqueline Wilson was doing a book-signing of her new book *Candyfloss* in Worthing, I was so excited that I ran to the bookshop to buy my copy. I read the book and adored it. I knew that I just had to get it signed.

In the queue to meet Jacqueline it was very cold but that didn't matter because I was so thrilled to meet her that adrenalin was rushing through my body at the speed of light. Once I got to the door I could see Jacqueline already and my heart skipped a beat as I realized that this was my deepest fantasy coming true. Jacqueline Wilson is my heroine; I always wanted to be just like her and still do.

I love to write and she inspired me to keep on writing even when things don't go as planned. Most famous writers and celebrities only want to talk about their achievements but Jacqueline cared about me and my interests.

It was the best thing that had happened to me in years and I would do anything to meet her and talk to her again. I was so nervous but I conquered my nerves in the end and just enjoyed the experience.

Jacqueline Wilson is the greatest person I have ever met and I would say that day was the most exhilarating day of my whole life and I wouldn't trade that memory for the world.

Jacqueline
the author

It's always exciting for me going to a book-signing! I get this lovely fizzy feeling as if I'm going to a special party. I always try to dress up a little, in my best black clothes. I know my hands will be very much on show so I wear a beautiful big ring on every finger. Perhaps they're not the most sensible things to wear for a long signing session but they're certainly a good talking point. I can let all of you have a good look at them and decide which one you like the best. I sometimes let someone try one or two of the rings on so they can see just how heavy they are!

I don't go to big book-signings by myself. I have lovely people to look after me. Mostly I go to bookshops with Naomi, my publicist. She's brilliant at calmly organizing everything. She's so clever too at knowing exactly when I need another cup of coffee and a biscuit or maybe a glass of wine and a few crisps. She's like a second daughter to me and a dear friend. When Naomi is busy at home with her family I travel with Mary, another lovely friend who works at Random House. She's also a fantastic organizer and, like me, a dedicated shopper.

35

If there's time we might squeeze in a spot of shopping on our day out.

I have the huge luxury of being driven by Bob in his silver Mercedes — how glamorous is that! Bob is an invaluable part of our team. He's always so cheery and chats to everyone in the queue. He's on his feet for hours — and then has to drive us home. If Bob is chauffeuring another author then I have Robbie instead, who is great fun and so big and broad that lots of children think he's my own special minder!

I like to arrive really early for an event so that I can meet all the bookshop staff, and sometimes there are special children who have won competitions so they get to meet me privately. No matter how early I arrive there's always a long queue outside the shop already. It makes me feel very grand drawing up in Bob's fantastic car. When I get out there's a big cry of 'There she is!' I give everyone a wave and say I hope they don't have to wait too long.

I have a strong cup of coffee before the signing starts so that I'm feeling totally wide awake. I make sure I nip to the loo because I will be sitting signing for many hours. Then I go to the desk and get started!

Each event always feels as if it really is a party. There are often balloons everywhere and staff offer sweets and give out special quizzes and people do face-painting. There's music playing and a happy buzz of chatter — although often you're struck dumb when you meet me! Don't worry, I know how weird it feels. But hopefully we can have a little chat while I'm signing your book. I love finding out what your name is. I keep note of some of the really special unusual names so that I can use them for characters in future books. I'm always touched that you've often dressed up too. It's such fun seeing what you're wearing. I take in your hairstyles too. I always wanted very long hair when I was a child so I'm always very envious of those of you with fairy princess long locks.

Of course it gets tiring signing for all those hours and if I try to eat or drink at the same time I often get hiccups! My hand aches, my back hurts, and I have dazzly lights in front of my eyes from all those photos. But it doesn't matter in the slightest. I'm still so happy to meet as many of you as possible. It gives me a chance to thank you for being such lovely loyal fans. It means so much to me that you — and your valiant parents, grannies, aunties, friends — are willing to wait hours to get your book signed.

Jacqueline Wilson

MAKE JACQUELINE'S FAVOURITE CAKE!

It wouldn't surprise anyone who knows her that Jacky's favourite cake is deeply, richly ultra-chocolaty. She got this recipe from Nick Sharratt's mum! Nick says a small slice of this gives him all the inspiration and energy he needs to tackle a new book and Jacqueline couldn't agree more. It is also Biscuits' cake from *Best Friends*! This is a huge cake and will be big enough to feed your whole class and still have some left over. There's no need to bake it – just mix it all up and leave it in the fridge to set.

CHOCOLATE BISCUIT CAKE

Ingredients

300g Rich Tea biscuits

250g unsalted butter

100g cocoa powder

300g icing sugar

3–4 tbs double cream

(Optional) Good handful of
halved glacé cherries or raisins
or stoned dates or a mixture
of these

You will also need:
A saucepan 1/3rd filled with hot water
and a large mixing bowl that will fit
into the top.

A 21–23cm spring form or loose-bottomed
cake tin.

METHOD

1. Line the cake tin with foil,
   smoothing it well into the
   sides and bottom and taking
   it a few centimetres above
   the sides. Lightly grease
   the foil with butter.

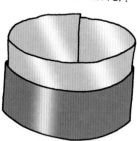

3. Sieve the icing sugar and
   cocoa and mix together
   in a bowl.
   Set aside.

2. Break the biscuits into
   small pieces and set aside.

4. Put the saucepan of hot water over a low heat and bring to a gentle simmer.

5. Cut the butter into small cubes and put into the large mixing bowl. Now place this bowl over the saucepan of water until the butter is completely melted. The bottom of the bowl should not touch the water.

6. Keeping the bowl over the gentle heat, add the sugar and cocoa mixture, two to three tablespoonfuls at a time, and stir vigorously but carefully, into the melted butter. Make sure that the mixture does not get too hot.

8. Now add the Rich Tea biscuit pieces to the chocolate mix and any optional ingredients such as cherries, etc. Stir with a wooden spoon until it is all coated with the chocolate sauce.

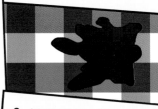

7. Remove the bowl from the heat and, using a wooden spoon, beat in the cream.

You should now have a rich, chocolaty sauce.

9. Scrape the chocolaty-biscuity mixture into the lined cake tin, pressing down with the back of the wooden spoon. Fold the excess foil gently over the top.

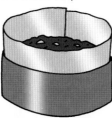

10. Put the cake in the refrigerator for several hours until set. Chill for at least 4 hours or overnight if possible. Serve in thin slices or small cubes. It is very rich!

How to have the Best-ever Super-cool Jacqueline Wilson Party

Got a birthday coming up? Half-term or school holidays round the corner? Get to grips with our guide on how to host the most fantastic, fun sleepover or party with a Jacqueline Wilson theme.

Want to do something less energetic but just as much fun when you get home? Give yourselves a makeover! Mandy is thrilled when Tanya does her hair and lets her try on her shoes in *Bad Girls*. Set out mirrors, brushes, hairspray and all your best clips, scrunchies and hair bands and take it in turns to transform each other. Perhaps you could also paint your nails with glittery colours to go with your glamorous new look?

Or get out all your pens, glitter, glue, tissue paper, coloured pencils and paper, or even some scraps of gorgeous fabrics, buttons, ribbons and sewing needles and threads and get creative, just like Violet in *Midnight*.

Make your invitations special by drawing your favourite Jacqueline Wilson characters on them. Maybe you can use envelopes in lots of different colours, just like Chloe does in *Sleepovers*? You could invite your friends to dress as their favourite Jacqueline Wilson characters too! Who'll come in special black trousers with a black-and-silver top, like Vicky Angel wears? Has anyone got short spiky hair and strappy high-heeled shoes like Tanya? And are any of your friends twins? Guess who they could come as!

Why not make your party special with an activity? Splash out at the local pool – it's brilliant fun, keeps you fit, gives you a great appetite for special party food afterwards – and swimming is Jacqueline Wilson's favourite sport. The pool's usually open all day – don't feel you have to get up for the Earlybirds club, just because Em does in *Clean Break*!

If your friends are coming for tea, why not try and have food based on your favourite books? You could have make-your-own pizzas, just like at Chloe's party in *Sleepovers*. All you need is some pizza bases, some tomato sauce for spreading on top, plenty of mozzarella cheese cut into slices and lots of interesting toppings, all ready to add. Try pieces of peppers in traffic-light colours, sliced mushrooms, olives, tuna, whatever you fancy . . .

You could drink delicious fruity cocktails decorated with paper umbrellas, like Amy has in *Sleepovers*. Or wonderful strawberry ice-cream sodas with long silver spoons and red straws, like Biscuits and Gemma drink in *Best Friends*.

If you're not too full after all that yummy food, why not make up your own dance routine? Pick your favourite music, push back the furniture and strut your funky stuff, just like Treasure and her nan in *Secrets*! If you choose country and western music and get your friends organised into a line, you might be just like Jacqueline herself at her line-dancing lessons!

If your friends are staying for a sleepover, let the fun continue even after you've snuggled down into your sleeping bags. Why not test each other with the fun quizzes in this book and find out who really is the greatest bookworm and dedicated Jacqueline Wilson fan?

And if it's your birthday perhaps your best friend could make Gemma's chocolate cake (like the one on page 35) as a delicious centre piece – just make sure you don't feel tempted to thrust it into any annoying girl's face!

Happy birthday, have fun and party on, everyone!

What do cannibals like for breakfast?
Buttered host.

What do Frenchmen eat for breakfast?
Huit heures bix.

What happens when a baby eats Rice Krispies?
It goes snap, crackle and poop.

What does Dracula like for breakfast?
Readyneck.

What do you get if you pour boiling water down a rabbit hole?
Hot cross bunnies!

How would a cannibal describe a man in a hammock?
Breakfast in bed.

A guest in a posh hotel calls the waiter. 'Can I order two boiled eggs, one under-cooked and runny, one overcooked and tough, and some rubbery bacon and burnt toast.'
The waiter says, 'Sir! We cannot serve such an awful breakfast!'
'Why not?' the guest replied.
'That's what I got here yesterday!'

What do ghosts like for breakfast?
Dreaded wheat.

What do cows eat for breakfast?
Moo-sli.

43

Would you DARE?

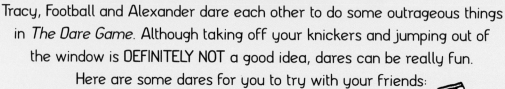

Tracy, Football and Alexander dare each other to do some outrageous things in *The Dare Game*. Although taking off your knickers and jumping out of the window is DEFINITELY NOT a good idea, dares can be really fun. Here are some dares for you to try with your friends:

You could try these ones at school

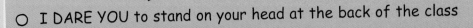

- ○ I DARE YOU to stand on your head at the back of the class
- ○ I DARE YOU to eat your school dinner in reverse – pudding first, then the main course – and finish every last mouthful
- ○ I DARE YOU to buy an ice cream and present it to a teacher.

You could try these ones at home

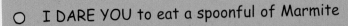

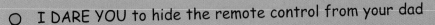

- ○ I DARE YOU to eat a spoonful of Marmite
- ○ I DARE YOU to hide the remote control from your dad

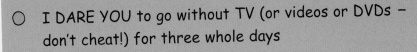

- ○ I DARE YOU to go without TV (or videos or DVDs – don't cheat!) for three whole days

You could try these ones in the park

◉ I DARE YOU to somersault round the perimeter of the park

○ I DARE YOU to run a circuit of the park backwards

○ I DARE YOU to find a spider and pick it up

You could try these ones at the weekend

○ I DARE YOU to wear your clothes backwards and act really surprised if anyone comments on it

○ I DARE YOU to announce you've changed your name for the day – and only answer to your new name

○ I DARE YOU to send a secret card to someone you like – even if it's not Valentine's Day

Today my name is Gloria!

Problems

A story by Jacqueline Wilson

Miss Drummond drones on and on about these awful maths problems. I can't understand maths even if I concentrate until the steam comes out of my ears. Besides, I've got other things on my mind. I doodle on the back of my maths book, writing my name all sorts of fancy ways and surrounding each posh squiggly signature with elaborately entwined flowers. Then I write down Damian Chatham. He's this boy I like in our class. He's not my boyfriend. I wish! Damian's not the most good-looking boy and he's not the cleverest and he's not the best at sport – but he's funny and kind and I like him lots, though I'm too shy to let on to anyone, apart from my friend Lucy.

I don't know if Damian likes me or not. He said he liked my long hair once. And another time when I dropped the ball in rounders and everyone groaned he said quietly, 'Don't worry, Nicola.' But that doesn't really mean any-thing. He's nice to everyone. He's nice to my friend Lucy.

She's nuts about him too.

There's a little poke in my back. I turn round. Lucy passes me a note, keeping a wary eye on Miss Drummond. I have a peek under my desk.

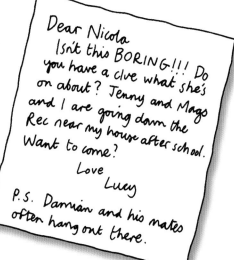

Dear Nicola
Isn't this BORING!!! Do you have a clue what she's on about? Jenny and Mags and I are going down the Rec near my house after school. Want to come?
Love
Lucy
P.S. Damian and his mates often hang out there.

I read Lucy's note. I read it again. I read the last line over and over. I want to go down to the rec with Lucy and Jenny and Mags – and maybe Damian! – soooo much. But I can't.

Dear Lucy, I write. *Sorry, I can't make it after school. Don't you dare get off with Damian yourself! I haven't got a clue about the Maths problems either. Old Drummond could be talking in some obscure Tuareg dialect for all I know—*

Lucy never gets my note because Miss Drummond stops her long involved mathematical discourse and sees me scribbling. She asks me what I'm writing. I say, 'Nothing, Miss Drummond.' She sighs, beckons, and holds out her hand. I have to give her the note. She raises her eyebrows at the Old Drummond Tuareg bit. I hold my breath.

I'm terrified she'll give me a detention. I have to get back home for Mum. They know a bit about her at school, but they don't know how bad things are now. They still think Dad's around anyway. We can't tell them in case they have to report it.

It's almost a relief when Miss Drummond sets me extra maths homework instead. I won't be able to do it, of course. I'll have to be suck up to Clever Clogs Chrissie and bribe her with the Kit-Kat from my packed lunch to see if she'll do the maths problems for me.

'Sorry you got caught, Nicks,' says Lucy, when the bell goes. 'You coming to the rec then?'

'I can't, Lucy.'

'You can. Look, I tell you, I heard Damian chatting to Jack and Liam and Little Pete. They're planning to play footie there.'

'You know I have to do the shopping for my mum.'

'Yeah, but you could do that after.'

'I can't be late for her.'

Lucy sighs. She knows about my mum and me. I've sworn her to secrecy. But she doesn't understand.

'You've got to have some life of your own, Nicola,' she says. Like it's a choice I can make.

Lucy's my best ever friend, but sometimes I feel like we're poles apart. She's at the North Pole spinning under the stars with Jenny and Mags and Jack and Liam and Little Pete and my Damian – and I'm down at the South Pole all by myself, unable to get hold of my own life.

I rush off without even saying goodbye properly. I don't want Lucy to see I've got tears in my eyes. I blink furiously and hurry down to Tesco and buy all the food and stuff. Then I have to go to Boots and stand at the counter with these big packs of incontinence pads. I should be used to it by now but I still go bright red, scared that people will think they're for me, though I know no-one can help being incontinent and it's nothing to be ashamed of.

I peer just for a moment in New Look but I haven't got time for a proper look and there's no point anyway. We haven't got any spare cash.

Then I lumber everything home. There's no bus that goes near our flats and taxis are out of the question. My arms ache and I feel hot and tired and fed up. I can't help thinking about Lucy and the girls down the rec, sitting on the swings, giggling away, watching Damian and the others kicking a football about. Then the ball gets kicked near them, Lucy catches it, Damian comes running over, they have a little laugh together, Lucy tosses her lovely shiny hair out of her eyes, Damian stares her, smiles . . . It's as if it's actually happening in front of me. It's not fair.

But it's stupid getting worked up about it. 'Stupid stupid stupid,' I hiss to myself as I go into our estate. I keep my eyes down and just nod quickly whenever anyone says hello. We can't have anyone getting too friendly and coming round. If they saw how bad Mum is now they'd maybe start interfering.

I have to trail up three flights of stairs because the lifts are broken again. Just as well we don't live right up on the fifteenth floor. Still, I don't suppose it makes much difference to Mum.

I stop in front of our front door. I wipe my eyes. I breathe deeply. I stretch my lips into a great big smile. Then I let myself in.

'Cooee, Mum,' I go, as I always do.

There's a little pause. My heart thumps – but then, faintly, 'Cooee, Nicky,' comes from the living room.

I dump the shopping in the hall and go to see her. She's got her bag open and a tissue in her hand. Maybe she was having a little weep herself? Her eyes look red. But she's got her own smile firmly fixed in place.

'Hi there, my best girl,' she says.

'Wotcha, my best mum,' I say. 'Cup of tea?'

'Yes please,' she says, but her smile slips. 'Oh, Nicky, if only I could have a cup of tea waiting for you, like a proper mum.'

'Oh, so are you an improper mum?' I say quickly, taking her lunchtime tray. She's tipped her cup over but she's started using one of those ones with a lid and a spout so it didn't spill. She's got sandwich crumbs all down her front though. She sees me looking and tries to brush them away but her hands are so feeble nowadays they're not much use. She tries so hard to keep herself nice but on a bad day she can't even brush her hair or do her own make-up. Some days she doesn't feel like it anyway. She just says, 'What's the point?' and sits and stares into space. Those are the scariest days.

My mum's got this progressive illness. It means she can't get better. She can only get worse. She can't manage more than a couple of steps now. She can't lift anything with her hands. She can't get to the loo in time. She can't even bath herself now.

Mum hasn't always been like this. She used to be fit and healthy and strong. Stronger than most mums. I remember one day when I was little and we were on holiday at the seaside. Mum and I were paddling together, holding hands, jumping the waves – but then a big wave came and I slipped and went under. I got scared but Mum scooped me up and whirled me round and round so that my toes skimmed the water and it was just like I was flying. We ran races along the sands later to get warm and Mum always beat me. She could even beat my dad.

He cleared off last year. He was OK when Mum was first diagnosed. She was just a bit clumsy and fell over every now and then. Dad helped her and said he was sure she'd get better in time. But she didn't get better, she gradually got worse. Dad cried the first time she had to use a wheelchair. He said it made him feel so bad. How did he think it made Mum feel?

Dad got more and more depressed and started staying out late. He said it was because he couldn't bear to watch Mum suffer. But he'd started seeing this woman at his work. He lives with her now. He still sends us money – well, most of the time. But he hardly ever comes to see us. Still, we manage fine without him.

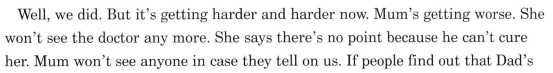

Well, we did. But it's getting harder and harder now. Mum's getting worse. She won't see the doctor any more. She says there's no point because he can't cure her. Mum won't see anyone in case they tell on us. If people find out that Dad's gone for good and I'm the only one looking after Mum then they might split us up. Mum would end up in a Home and I'd end up in Care.

We couldn't bear that. We've got to stay together no matter what. So it's like I've taken over. I'm like the mum and she's like my little baby. I do everything for her. I don't want to. I get fed up lots of times. But what else can I do?

I know that one day Mum will get so bad she won't be able to be left. I don't know what I'm going to do then. I've thought about dashing home at lunch time, or bunking off school altogether, but then they'd investigate.

It's like one of Miss Drummond's maths problems. I can't seem to come up with any answer. And sometimes when Lucy goes on and on about life being so unfair because her mum won't buy her this new leather jacket or her dad won't let her go to a party I just stare at her and think, If only I had your problems, Lucy. But I don't go on at her. Lucy's my friend. Even if she does get off with Damian.

I think about them as I make Mum's tea and sort her out. I think about them as Mum and I watch telly while we eat. I think about them as I do the dishes and put the sheets in the washing machine and start on yesterday's ironing.

Then the phone rings.

It'll be Lucy. All set to show off. Telling me about her and Damian.

'Nicky? It won't be for me,' calls Mum.

'Oh, I'm busy, Mum,' I yell from the kitchen. 'It doesn't matter. Just let it ring.'

It rings and rings. I hear Mum grunt as she drags herself sideways, reaching out for it with one shaky hand.

'Don't, Mum!' I shout – but she's already answering.

'Nicky?' Mum calls. 'Someone to speak to you.'

I sigh. I close my eyes. I practise saying, 'Good for you, Lucy. Sure, it's cool with me. I hope you and Damian are very happy.'

But it's not Lucy. When I trudge into the living room Mum mouths at me, 'It's a boy!' She grins at my shocked face.

My hands are shaking as I snatch the phone.

'Hi, Nicola. It's me, Damian.'

I swallow. I say 'Hi' back in such a silly squeak he doesn't hear me.

'Nicola?'

'Hello, Damian.'

'I've just been at the Rec with my mates.'

'Oh. Yeah?'

'And Lucy and them were there too.'

Oh no, he's going to tell me that they've made friends.

'Right,' I say tensely.

'I hoped you might be there too.'

'Oh. No. I . . . I had things to do.'

'Yes, Lucy said that. I asked her for your phone number. I hope that's all right?'

'Mmm.' My heart is beating so fast I'm sure he can hear it.'

'Lucy said your mum's not well and you have to do the shopping and that?'

'Yes.'

'Well, maybe . . . maybe I could help you with the shopping sometimes?'

'With your mates?'

'No! Just you and me. I could help you carry the bags. If you'd like?'

'Oh. Well.' Thank goodness I've just stocked up at Boots! But I suppose it wouldn't matter if he came round Tesco with me. In fact, it would be wonderful.

Mum is looking at me, nodding determinedly.

'Say YES!' she mouths.

'OK then. Yes. If you're sure you wouldn't mind.'

'I'd like to. OK? Well, see you at school tomorrow and we'll maybe go shopping after.'

'Yes. Damian? Thanks for phoning.'

I put the phone down, dazed. Mum's smile is real this time, from one ear to the other.

'Oh, Nicky, he sounds so sweet. Now look, after you go shopping together go to McDonald's, right?'

'But Mum, I can't. You'll be waiting.'

'And I can wait a bit longer. I just want you to have a little bit of fun, sweet-heart. Goodness knows, you deserve it. You have to do so much for me.'

'And I always will, Mum,' I say.

I give her a big hug and just at this moment I'm so happy I feel strong enough to scoop her up out of danger and whirl her round and round and keep her flying for ever.

THE END

Do you recognize any of these memorable birthday celebrations?

'Happy birthday, Gemma darling,' said Mum, giving me a kiss.

She handed me a pink tissue parcel tied with a polka-dot ribbon. I shook it for clues.

'Careful!' said Mum.

I saw the word MAKE-UP faintly showing through the pink tissue. Oh dear, it looked like Mum had taken me seriously about wanting to be girly. I tried to pin a smile on my face as I ripped the tissue off. Then I smiled properly, a great grin from ear to ear. It wasn't ordinary girly pink lippy and peach powder. It was a box of stage make-up, with all kinds of colour sticks, zingy oranges and crimsons, wild greens and greys and deep blues. I stared at the sticks and saw myself made up as the Incredible Hulk, Spiderman, Dracula, the Lion King . . . My starring roles were endless. There was even a stick of black to make an excellent Fat Larry moustache.

Mum and Steve woke me up singing 'Happy Birthday to you'. They'd stuck candles in a big fat croissant and put a little paper umbrella and a cocktail stick of cherries in my orange juice.

My little half-brother Tiger came crawling into my bedroom too. He's too tiny to sing but he made a loud he-he-he noise, sitting up on his padded bottom and clapping his hands. He's really called Tim, but Tiger suits him better.

I blew out all my candles. Tiger cried when the flames went out, so we had to light them all again for him to huff and puff at.

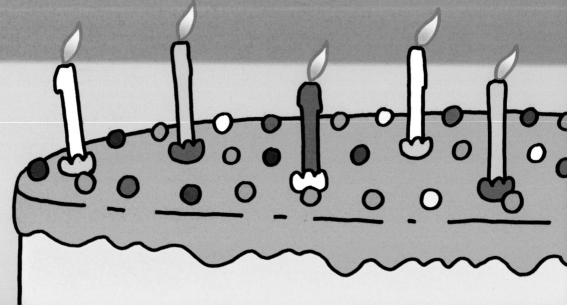

Well, I'd have my own house, right? And I'd employ someone to foster me. But because I'd be paying them, they'd have to do everything I said. I'd order them to make me a whole birthday cake to myself every single day of the week and they'd just have to jump to it and do so.

I wouldn't let anybody else in to share it with me.

Not even Peter. I had to share my real birthday cake with him. And he gave me a nudge and said, 'What's the matter, Tracy? Don't you feel well?' just when I'd closed my eyes tight and was in the middle of making my birthday wish. So it got all muddled and I lost my thread and now if my mum doesn't come for me it's all that Peter Ingham's fault.

Well, maybe it is.

But I'd still let him come round to my house sometimes and we could play paper games. They're quite good fun really, because I always win.

I had my birthday breakfast in bed. Mum and Steve perched at the end, drinking coffee. Tiger went exploring under my bed and came out all fluffy, clutching one of my long-forgotten socks. He held it over his nose like a cuddle blanket, while Mum and Steve cooed at his cuteness.

Then I got to open my presents. They were wrapped up in shiny silver paper with big pink bows. I thought they looked so pretty I just wanted to hold them for a moment, smoothing the silver paper and fingering the bows, trying to guess what might be inside. But Tiger started ripping them himself, tearing all the paper and tangling the ribbon.

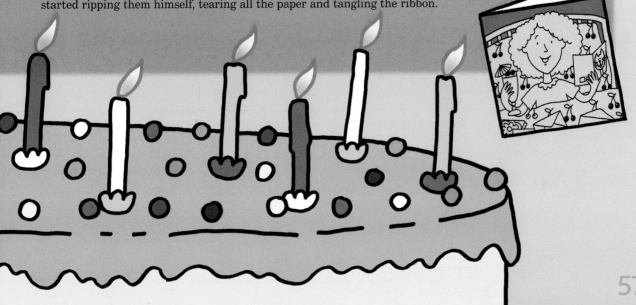

My Favourite Books

by Jacqueline Wilson

My favourite book when I was a child was *Nancy and Plum* by Betty MacDonald. It's sadly not widely available in England any more but it might just be possible to find a copy on Amazon. Nancy and Plum are two orphaned sisters stuck in a children's home run by hateful Mrs Monday. Nancy is a shy, dreamy girl of ten, with long red plaits. Plum is a fierce, funny girl of eight, with short fair plaits. They play all sorts of inventive, imaginary games together and love reading.

I adored the chapters where they fantasize about the dolls they'd like for Christmas and choose their favourite books from the library. They decide to run away and eventually find a wonderful new home on a farm with Mr and Mrs Campbell, who give them lots of love and hugs and treats. They get pets and dolls and party frocks and black patent shoes and Mrs Campbell bakes them wonderful homemade pies every day. I read *Nancy and Plum* again and again as a child. I made up my own Nancy and Plum imaginary games, pretending they were my sisters. When my daughter Emma was about seven I read her the story, and she loved it just as much as I did.

I loved lots of other books which luckily are still in print so you can see for yourself how good they are.

I liked *Ballet Shoes* by Noel Streatfeild – about three orphaned sisters this time! Pauline, Petrova and Posy get to go to stage school. Pauline is the pretty one who loves acting. Petrova is plain and hates having to prance about on stage – she wants to fly planes. Posy is a little show-off who is seriously gifted at ballet. They are such true-to-life, realistic girls. I used to imagine I was at stage school with them and pretended my pink bedroom slippers were ballet shoes!

Ballet Shoes seemed a bit old-fashioned even when I was a child but I didn't mind a bit. I loved Victorian stories like *Little Women* by Louisa M. Alcott, about four sisters, Meg, Jo, Beth and Amy. I liked Jo best, because she was the most lively, an untidy tomboy who loved reading and writing her own stories. I also loved *What Katy Did* by Susan Coolidge. Katy is the oldest and naughtiest child in a very large family. She has a fall from a swing and is in bed, unable to walk, for a very long time. She naturally grumbles and complains but then she has a visit from her saintly cousin Helen who helps her to be good. She's not quite so much fun then!

You might have read *The Secret Garden* by Frances Hodgson Burnett at school, and it's a lovely book, but I prefer another story by the same author, *A Little Princess*. Sara is a rich little girl who is left at boarding school by her loving father, and given all sorts of splendid things, even an entire wardrobe of elaborate clothes for her precious new doll Emily. Sara isn't spoiled though, she's a very kind, imaginative girl, who makes friends with Becky the serving maid. Then Sara's father dies and Sara herself has no money left and has to work as a maid in the school herself. She's half-starved and treated cruelly, but she's got tremendous spirit and keeps going somehow. Of course there's a lovely fairy-tale ending!

THE LIFE OF A JACQUELINE WILSON BOOK

Jacqueline's books always start their life as scribbled stories in one of the notebooks that she carries with her at all times. Jacqueline is so busy that she often snatches time to work on her books on trains or in cars, rushing from one event or meeting to another. She writes three or four pages at a time, sometimes stopping right in the middle of an exciting part – so she can get started easily the next day.

Jacky's notebook

As soon as she has time Jacqueline then types out the story on her computer, which is a big change for her as until a few years ago she was still using a typewriter. Once she has printed it out, Jacqueline reads through it, makes a few corrections and checks that all the pages are there. As she still doesn't quite trust the computer to do it, she then numbers each page by hand.

Then she posts it off to her literary agent and her editors at the publishing house, who can't wait to rush home and read it – just like any Jacky fan would. The editors send a copy to Nick Sharratt so he can start thinking about what to draw for the cover and any inside pictures.

Nick comes up with ideas

marked-up manuscript

> My Dad came and visited us in hospital. Fathers didn't get involved much with
>
> babies in those days but he held me gently in his big broad hands and gave me a kiss.
>
> My Grandma caught the train from Kingston up to London, where we lived, and then she got on a
> she took
> tube, and then the Paddington train to Bath and then a bus to the hospital, just to catch a
>
> glimpse of her new grand-daughter. It must have taken her practically all day to get there
>
> because transport was slow and erratic just after the war.

Once the editors have read it, they usually have a few small suggestions for Jacky about how the story might be altered, for example, making one episode longer and more detailed or changing the name of a character if it's too similar to one in a previous book. When the final version of the story is agreed between Jacky and the editors, the manuscript is checked by a copy-editor. This person makes sure all the punctuation, grammar and spelling in the book is correct and checks that everything makes sense too.

A designer at the publishing house decides how each page of the book should look – for example which font to use for the writing and how many lines to have on each page. Then the manuscript is sent to a typesetter, where the whole text is typed out and arranged on the pages according to the instructions from the designer. The pages, known as proofs, are then sent back to the publishing house. They are read by two editors and Jacqueline to make sure that no mistakes have crept in at the typesetter's and that everything is perfect. It's also a final chance for Jacky and her editors to check they're absolutely happy with the story. Despite three different people doing this proofreading, tiny mistakes can still be missed – and sometimes eagle-eyed fans spot them once the book is published and write in to tell the publisher.

cover variations

While all this work is being done on the text, Nick will have designed a cover and sent in a rough sketch of it. The picture, colours and special extras to be used, such as shiny foils or matt finishes, are discussed in detail. Once Jacqueline, Nick and the publishers are all agreed, Nick sends in final artwork on disk to the designer. The editor writes the 'blurb' or description for the jacket of the book. All these bits are put together by the designer and then the production controller sends it to a reproduction house. The picture is separated out into four colours (cyan, magenta, yellow and black) from which the cover proofs are made.

Meanwhile Nick gets on with drawing any pictures that are to appear inside the book. When the illustrations, covers and text are all ready, a disk is sent to the printer, who puts it all together and makes the books!

Jacky Daydream
cover design

disk ↗

The paper for the books is on huge rolls and it's only once the words and pictures are printed on it that the pages can be folded to the right size and cut to separate them. The pages are then bound together (usually with glue) and stuck inside the cover, which is folded around them. The printing presses work extremely fast, making 2,500 books an hour.

Photographs courtesy of William Clowes Limited.

As soon as the first few copies are ready they are sent to the publishing house, where the editor forwards one straight to Jacky and to Nick. This is one of the most exciting moments in the whole process – the first sight of a brand-new Jacqueline Wilson novel!

Once the printer has printed all the copies ordered by the publisher – and for the first printing of a brand-new Jacky book in hardback that's normally about 150,000 copies — they are boxed and delivered by lorry to the warehouse.

In the warehouses the boxes are coded so that as soon as an order is received from a bookshop, school or library the correct book can be found and delivered to the right place. Then it can be bought or borrowed by you and you can rush home to curl up with a fantastic new book to enjoy.

So you think
you know about

SCHOOL

in Jacqueline
Wilson's books?

SIT DOWN, TAKE OUT
YOUR PENS, NO TALKING
PLEASE, AND REMEMBER
TO ANSWER ALL THE
QUESTIONS! THEN CHECK
YOUR ANSWERS AT THE
BACK OF THE BOOK.

$$\begin{array}{r} 20 \\ \times 12 \\ \hline 240 \end{array}$$

Charlie

1. In *Candyfloss* what is Susan's
   best subject at school?

2. What work do Susan's parents do?

3. Which other classmates does Rhiannon
   become friends with instead of Floss?

4. What nickname do Ruby and Garnet give the
   boy in their class called Jeremy Treadgold?

$$\begin{array}{r} 87 \\ -17 \\ \hline 70 \end{array}$$

5. What topic is Charlie learning about when
   she does the Lottie Project?

6. In *Midnight*, which play has Violet been
   studying at school just before Jasmine
   joins her class?

$$\begin{array}{r} 119 \\ -15 \\ \hline 104 \end{array}$$

7. Who offers to sit next to Gemma in class
   after Alice has left, in *Best Friends*?

8. In *Best Friends*, what project does Mrs Watson set the class?

9. Whom do Biscuits and Gemma feature in their project?

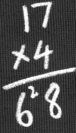

10. In *Clean Break*, what does Dad give Em to take to school to help her make friends?

11. What does Em do after school?

12. What is the name of Vicky and Jade's teacher in *Vicky Angel*?

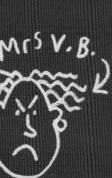

13. What's the full nickname that Tracy Beaker has given to the teacher she refers to as Mrs V.B.?

14. Which play is being staged at school in *Starring Tracy Beaker*?

15. What do Mike and Jenny make Tracy do at the Dumping Ground, when she's in trouble for hitting Justine?

Magical Makeovers

Are you feeling creative? Want to make your own personal space just that little bit more special? You could have a go at making over your room just like your favourite Jacqueline Wilson character! But don't forget to ask your parent or guardian before you start any radical redecorating. Apart from anything else, wouldn't you rather they carried the heavy paint tins all the way home from the DIY shop?!

There are as many different styles as there are characters in the books, but here are just a few ideas. Which one of these appeals to you the most?

Creative and unusual

In *The Illustrated Mum*, Marigold has transformed Dolphin and Star's bedroom into a tropical sea topped by a starry galaxy, using just a few cans of paint and a lot of talent and imagination. All the walls and the ceiling are painted in deep blue as a background. There are ocean scenes on the walls showing whales, sharks, a coral reef, mermaids and, of course, a whole school of dolphins. On the ceiling is the night sky, showing all the stars of the Milky Way.

If you or a relative or friend have got pots of talent – and pots of paint – you could turn your bedroom into an aquarium or planetarium like this. Or into whatever else takes your fancy. Emulsion paint for walls and ceilings is available in every imaginable colour – and then some more!

Strong colour scheme

If you really love one colour, make the most of it! In *The Lottie Project*, Charlie's favourite colour is red and in the bedroom she shares with her mum they've got dark-red paint on the walls, crimson curtains they found in a car-boot sale and a purply-red lamp. On special occasions, Charlie and her mum make a fantastic red picnic (with cherries, plums, jam tarts, Ribena and so on) and take it back to their red room.

Express your personality

If you get the chance, it's great to be able to stamp your own personality on your bedroom. Whether it's just a collection of prized possessions on one shelf or a complete theme based on your favourite hobby, it can be a way of showing what's important to you. You'll feel truly comfortable there and it'll instantly show your friends and family that it's your place.

In *Bad Girls*, Mandy has her special collection of 22 toy monkeys arranged on shelves and on the floor in her room.

In *Midnight*, Violet has hung her 14 handmade fairies from her ceiling. She's sewn them herself, based on the drawings in her favourite books.

Ultra-girly

If your dream room is a pink palace, you can model it on Alice's bedroom in her new house, in *Best Friends*. Alice has a pale-pink carpet with a deep-pink rug in the shape of a rose beside her bed. The duvet cover and pillow case are white with pink roses. Alice's old wardrobe and chest of drawers have been painted rose-pink to match and she has a new pink desk with her gel pens on top of it (guess what colour they are!).

Alice's best friend Gemma isn't all that impressed but for some girls this would be bedroom heaven!

Making the best of it

In *The Dare Game*, Tracy Beaker's new friend Alexander has managed to create a sense of fun and cosiness in the most basic of rooms in an abandoned, empty house. The muddy, ancient sofa has been covered with a blanket and he's added a black velvet cushion. He's used an upturned packing case as a table, covering it with a cheerful checked tea towel, like a tablecloth. As far as Tracy's concerned, the best touch is that on the top of the cloth is a paper plate full of Smarties, arranged in rings by colour!

67

Get stuck into a good book

We know what YOU like reading – but what about the characters in your favourite books? What do they choose in the library?

I wandered around the shelves, picking up this book and that book, turning over the pages for the pictures. I could read, sort of, but I hated all those thick wodges of print. The words all wiggled on the page and wouldn't make any kind of sense. I looked to see if Mr Harrison was watching me but he was deep in his paper. I knelt down and poked my way through the picture books for little kids. There was a strange slightly scary one with lots of wild monsters. Marigold would have loved to turn them into a big tattoo. I liked a bright happy book too about a mum and a dad. The colours glowed inside the neat lines of the drawing. I traced round them with my finger. I tried to imagine what it would be like living in a picture-book world where monsters quelled by a look and you feel safe back in your own bed and you have a spotty mum and a stripy dad with big smiles on their pink faces and they make you laugh.

'What are you reading?'

'Nothing!' I said, shoving both books back on the shelf quickly.

But it was only Owly Morris. He wouldn't tease me for looking at picture books.

The Illustrated Mum

Jacky FACT

Jacqueline's first ever story featured the Maggott family and was written in an exercise book

This is the book about the spotty Mum and stripey Dad that Dolphin finds in the library. It's by Nick Sharratt!

They've got books in absolutely every room, even the downstairs loo, and there are shelves in the hall and the living room downstairs, but there's this huge great room on the first floor absolutely crammed full of books, and there are shelves and shelves of Victorian stuff.

'See,' said Jamie proudly, pulling various volumes down and displaying them in front of me.

I saw. No wonder Jamie's Victorian project was so brilliant. Still, he was letting me look at the books if I wanted.

I'd found a whole set of Victorian girls' books. I wanted to see if there might be any Lottie could have read. There was one huge fat annual with lots of pictures, like a magazine. There was one coloured picture of a huge table groaning with wobbly jellies and puddings like castles and all sorts of dinky sweets and teeny sandwiches . . . and fancy cakes.

'Hey, look! I just want to take a couple of notes, OK?'

'OK. Though why don't you borrow it?'

'You mean I can take it home with me?'

'Sure.'

'Oh. Well. Great.' I tucked the huge book under my arm. 'So let's play War.'

The Lottie Project

We sat cross-legged on the library floor while Susan built me a book house. I copied her, and then started making an elaborate tall block of flats. We turned our fingers into people and made them walk in between the houses and climb all the stairs to the high

rooftop of the flats. Then the library door opened suddenly and we both got such a fright that we jumped, and the book block of flats juddered and fell to the ground with a great clatter and crash.

Miss Van Dyke stood glaring at us. Miss Van Dyke, the deputy head, the scariest strictest old bat teacher in the entire school!

'What on *earth* are you doing, you two girls! This is a library, not a nursery playroom. What a way to treat books! Why aren't you in your classroom? First lesson started twenty minutes ago! Now put those books back this minute — carefully! — and then come with me. You're in Mrs Horsefield's class, aren't you?'

Candyfloss

The Violet Fairy from Jacqueline Wilson's *Midnight*

My Favourite Artists

by Jacqueline Wilson

My dad once took me to the National Gallery in London when I was a little girl. I stepped from the grey wintry day outside into a fantastic warm world of colour. I loved the blue of all the many Madonnas, the gold of the angels' haloes, the vivid velvety green of the Arnolfini lady's dress. I've loved going to art galleries ever since.

Prudence in my book *Love Lessons* is taken to the National Gallery by her father. She's bowled over too.

> *I didn't say much either. I was flying through this new magical world of religious Renaissance painting, so pink and blue and glittery gold. It was as if I'd sprouted my own beautiful set of angel's wings. I'd always painted wings plain white, but now I saw they could be shaded from the palest pearl through deep rose and purple to the darkest midnight-blue tips.*

Ellie in *Girls Under Pressure* goes to the National Gallery too. Her little brother Eggs thinks Tintoretto's *The Origin of the Milky Way* is very rude. I remember finding the naked lady in the clouds astonishingly rude too when I was about six, but now I think it's a fantastic painting. Ellie is too caught up agonizing over dieting herself stick-thin to appreciate the paintings, though she's a very artistic girl herself. Her favourite artist is Frida Kahlo — and I love Frida's savage strange South American art too. She nearly always paints herself, her dark hair piled up and decked with flowers, huge rings on every finger. She sometimes includes her pet parrots and monkeys in her paintings.

Ellie's art teacher Mr Windsor introduces her to the powerful art of Paula Rego. Ellie has her doubts at first because Paula Rego doesn't paint slim simpering conventional beauties but Mr Windsor's enthusiasm wins her over.

> 'They're big women, they're strong, they've got sturdy thighs, real muscles in their arms and legs. But they're soft too, they're vulnerable, they're valiant.'

I love Paula Rego just as much as Mr Windsor. Her art is disconcerting and amazing. If you go to the National Gallery, look at Paula Rego's wonderful mural in the restaurant called Crivelli's Garden. She does very special illustrations for books too. She did her own version of *Peter Pan* and I have her engraving of Wendy and a very savage-looking mermaid above my desk. I've been lucky enough to go to her studio and see all the dolls and models and strange clothes that appear in her paintings.

Ellie's self-portrait, inspired by her National Gallery visit

I've also been to wonderful Peter Blake's studio, a magical, ordered fairyland of bright toys and ornaments. I have one of his fantastic collages and one of my most treasured books is a signed copy of his *Alice through the Looking Glass*. I love his paintings of dreamy girls with long hair.

The Belgian artist Paul Delvaux also specializes in dreamy girls. His are all moon-pale and ethereal, wandering along railway tracks or lounging under Roman columns. Every painting looks as if it's illustrating an extraordinary dream.

I'm especially fond of Victorian art. Lots of artists specialised in painting fairies then. Violet in my book *Midnight* is obsessed with fairies and I invented an artist called Caspar Dream to entrance her. She pores over his illustrations just as I can gaze at the crazy detailed fairyland of Richard Dadd for hours, always finding some new astonishing detail. I also like the much smaller imaginative fairy paintings of John Anster Fitzgerald.

My favourite Victorian painters are the Pre-Raphaelites, a group of friends who painted very vividly and realistically, often choosing poems or plays or stories as their subject. I have many Pre-Raphaelite reproductions in my house. I love Millais's Ophelia floating down her green flower-filled stream (the same stream still flows at the bottom of my road!). Many stunning Rossetti women pose in paintings up and down my hall, their long wavy hair hanging way past their waists, and pale, mournful Burne-Jones nymphs droop languidly above my fireplace.

ODD ONE OUT

A story by Jacqueline Wilson

I'm the odd one out in the family. There are a lot of us. OK, here goes. There's my mum and my stepdad Graham and my big brother Mark and my big sister Ginnie and my little sister Jess and my big step brother Jon and my big stepsister Alice and then there's my little half-sister Cherry and my baby half-brother Rupert. And me, Laura. Not to mention my real dad's new baby and his girlfriend Gina's twins, but they live in Cornwall now so I only see them for holidays. Long holidays, like summer and sometimes Christmas and Easter. Not short bank holidays, like today. It's a bank holiday and that means an Outing.

I hate Outings. I like Innings. My idea of bliss would be to read my book in bed with a packet of Pop Tarts for breakfast, get up late and draw or colour or write stories, have bacon sandwiches and crisps and a big cream cake or two for lunch, read all afternoon, have a whole chocolate swiss roll for tea in front of the telly, draw or colour or write more stories, and then pizza for supper.

I've never enjoyed a day like that. It wouldn't work anyway because there are far too many of us if we all stay indoors, and the big ones hog the sofa and the comfy chairs and the little ones are always dashing around and yelling and grabbing my felt tips. And Mum is always trying to stop me eating all the food I like best, pretending that a plate of lettuce and carrots and celery is just as yummy as pizza (!) and Graham is always suggesting I might like to get on this bike he bought me and go for a ride.

I wish he'd get on his bike. And take the whole family with him. And most of mine. Imagine if it was just Mum and me . . .

We had to do a piece of autobiographical writing at school last week on 'My Family'. I pondered for a bit. Just writing down the names of my family would take up half the page. I wanted to write a proper story, not an autobiographical list. So I had an imaginary cull of my entire family apart from Mum and wrote about our life together as a teeny-weeny two-people family. I went into painstaking detail, writing about birthdays and Christmas and how my mum sometimes produced presents that had *Love from Daddy* or *Best Wishes from Auntie Kylie in Australia* – although I knew she'd really bought them herself. I even pretend-ed that Mum sometimes played at being my gran or even grandpa and I played at being her son or her little baby. I wrote that although we played these games it was just for fun. We weren't lonely at all. We positively loved being such a small family.

Mrs Mann positively loved my effort too! This was a surprise because Mrs Mann is very, very strict. She's the oldest teacher at school and she can be really scary and sarcastic. You can't mess around in Mrs Mann's class. She wears these neat grey suits that match her grey hair and white blouses with tidily tied bows and a pearl brooch precisely centred on her lapel. You can tell just by looking at her that she's a stickler for punctuation and spelling and paragraphing and all those other boring, boring, boring things that stop you getting on with the story. 'My Family' piece had its fair share of mistakes ringed in Mrs Mann's red rollerball but she still gave me a ten out of ten because she said it was such a vivid, truthful piece of heartfelt writing.

I felt a little fidgety about this. Vivid it might be, but truthful it wasn't. When Mrs Mann was talking about my small family, my friends Amy and Kate stared at me open-mouthed because I'm always whining on to them about my big family. Luckily they're not tell-tales.

Sometimes I get on better with all my Steps. My big stepbrother Jon likes art too and he always says sweet things about my drawings. My big stepsister Alice isn't bad either. One day when we were all bored she did my hair in these cool little plaits with beads and ribbons and made up my face so I looked almost grown up. Yes, I like Jon and Alice, but they're much older than me so they don't really want me hanging out with them.

The Halfies aren't bad either. I quite like sitting Cherry on my lap and reading her *Where the Wild Things Are*. She always squeals when I roar their terrible roars right in her ear and Mum gets cross but Cherry likes it. Rupert isn't into books yet – in fact I was a bit miffed when I showed him my old nursery-rhyme book and he bit it, like he thought it was a big bright sandwich. He's not really fun to play with yet because he's too little.

That's the trouble. Mark and Ginnie and Jon and Alice are too big. Jess and Cherry and Rupert are too little. I'm the Piggy in the Middle.

Hmm. My unpleasant brother Mark frequently makes grunting snorty noises at me and calls me Fatty Pigling.

I have highly inventive nicknames for Mark indeed, for all my family (apart from Mum) but I'd better not write them down or you'll be shocked.

I said a few very rude words to myself when Mum and Graham said we were going for a l-o-n-g walk along the river for our bank holiday outing. It's OK for Rupert. He goes in the buggy. It's OK for Cherry and Jess. They get piggyback rides the minute they start whining. It's OK for Mark and Ginnie and Jon and Alice. They stride ahead in a little gang (or lag behind, whatever) and they talk about music and football and s-e-x, and whenever I edge up to them they say, 'Push off, Pigling' if they're Mark or Ginnie, or, 'Hi, Laura, off you go now' if they're Jon or Alice.

I'd love it if it could just be Mum and me going on a walk together. But Graham is always around and he makes silly jokes or slaps me on the back or bosses me about. Sometimes I get really narked and tell him he's not my dad so he can't tell me what to do. Other times I just look at him. Looks can be very effective.

My face was contorted in a dark scowl all the long, long, long trudge along the river. It was so incredibly boring. I am past the age of going 'Duck duck duck' whenever a bird with wings flies past. I am not yet of the age to collapse into giggles when some dark-shaded male language students say hello in sexy foreign accents (Ginnie and Alice) and I don't stare gape-mouthed when a pretty girl in a bikini waves from a boat (Mark and Jon).

I just stomped around wearily, surreptitiously eating a Galaxy . . . and then a Kit-Kat . . . and a couple of Rolos. I handed the rest round to the family like a good generous girl. That's another huge disadvantage of large families. Offer your packet of Rolos round once and they're nearly all gone in one fell swoop.

We went to this pub garden for lunch and I galloped down a couple of cheese toasties and two packets of crisps and two Cokes – all this fresh air had made me peckish – and I had to stoke myself up for the long trail back home along the river.

'Oh, we thought we'd go via the Green Fields,' said Graham.

I groaned. 'Graham! It's miles! And I've got serious blisters already.'

'I think you might like the Green Fields this particular Monday,' said Mum.

She and Graham smiled.

I didn't smile back. I don't like the Green Fields. They are just what their name implies. Two big green fields joined by a line of poplar trees. They don't even have a playground with swings. There isn't even an ice-cream van. There's just a lot of grass.

But guess what, guess what! When we got nearer the Green Fields I heard this buzz and clatter and music and laughter. And then I smelled wonderful mouth-watering fried onions. We turned the corner – and the Green Fields were so full you couldn't see a glimpse of grass! There was a fair there for the bank holiday.

I gave a whoop. Mark and Ginnie and Jon and Alice gave a whoop too, though they were half mocking me. Jess and Cherry gave great big whoops. Baby Rupert whooped too. He couldn't see the fair down at kneecap level in his buggy but he didn't want to be left out.

Mum and Graham smiled smugly.

Of course, the fair meant different things to all of us. Jon and Mark – and Graham – wanted to go straight on the dodgems. Ginnie and Alice and I went too, while Mum minded the littlies. She bought them all whippy ice creams with chocolate flakes. I wailed, saying I'd much much much sooner have an ice cream than get in a dodgem car. Mum sighed and bought me an ice cream too. But as soon as it was in my hand I decided it might be fun to go on the dodgems too, so I jumped in beside Jon.

Big mistake. Mark drove straight into us, *wham bam* and then *splat*, the chocolate flake went right up my nostril and my ice cream went all over my face.

Mum mopped me up with one of Rupert's wetwipes, and Jon bought me another ice cream to console me. I licked this in peace while Jess and Cherry and baby Rupert sat in a kiddies' roundabout and slowly and solemnly revolved in giant teacups.

'I wonder if they've got a proper roundabout,' said Mum. 'I used to love those ones with the horses and the twisty gilt rails and the special music. I want to go on a real old-fashioned carousel.'

'Oh, Mum, you don't get those any more,' said Ginnie – but she was wrong.

We went on all sorts of new-fashioned rides first. We were all hurtled round and round and upside down until even I started wondering if that extra ice cream had been a good idea. Then, as we staggered queasily to the other side of the field, we heard old organ music. Mum lifted her head, listening intently.

'Is it?' she said.

It was. We pushed through the crowd and suddenly it was just like stepping back a hundred years. There was the most beautiful old roundabout with galloping horses with grinning mouths and flaring nostrils and scarlet saddles, some shiny black, some chocolate brown, some dappled grey. There was also one odd pink ostrich with crimson feathers and an orange beak.

'Why is that big bird there, Mum?' I asked.

'I don't know, Laura. I think they always have one odd one. Maybe it's a tradition.'

'I'm going to go on the bird,' I said.

The roundabout was slowing down. Mum had little Rupert unbuckled from his buggy so he could ride too. Graham had Cherry in his arms. Mark and Jon said the roundabout was just for kids, but when Graham asked one of them to look after Jess they both offered eagerly. Ginnie and Alice had an argument over who was going to ride on a black horse with Robbie on his nameplate (they both have a thing about Robbie Williams) so eventually they squeezed on together.

I rushed for the ostrich. I didn't need to. No-one else wanted it. Well, I did. I clambered on and stroked its crimson feathers. Ostriches are definitely the odd ones out of the bird family. They can't fly. They're too heavy for their own wings.

I'm definitely the odd one out of my family – and I frequently feel too heavy for my own legs. I sat gripping the ostrich with my knees, waiting for the music to start and the round-about to start revolving. People were still scrabbling onto the few remaining horses. A middle-aged lady in much too tight jeans was hauling this little toddler up onto the platform. I put out my hand to help – and then stopped, astonished. I couldn't have been more amazed if my ostrich had opened its beak and bitten me. It wasn't any old middle-aged lady bursting out of her jeans. It was Mrs Mann!

I stared at her – and she stared at me.

'Hello, Laura,' she said. 'This is my little granddaughter Rosie.'

I made appropriate remarks to Rosie while Mrs Mann struggled to get them both up onto the ordinary brown horse beside my splendid ostrich. Mrs Mann couldn't help showing rather a lot of her vast blue-denimed bottom. I had to struggle to keep a straight face.

'Are you with your mother, Laura?' said Mrs Mann.

Oh help! Mum was in front of me with Rupert. I had written Mrs Mann that long essay about Mum and me just living together. I hadn't mentioned any babies whatsoever.

'I'm here . . . on my own,' I mumbled.

At that exact moment Mum turned round and waved at me.

'Are you all right, Laura?' she called. She nodded at Mrs Mann.

Mum and Mrs Mann looked at me, waiting for me to introduce them. I stayed silent as the music started up. *Go, go, go* I urged inside my head. But we didn't go soon enough.

'I'm Laura's mum,' said Mum.

'I'm Laura's teacher,' said Mrs Mann. 'And this is Rosie.'

Rosie waved coyly to Rupert.

'This is my baby Rupert,' said Mum.

Mrs Mann looked surprised.

'And that's Cherry over there with my partner Graham and Jess with my son Mark and that's my stepson Jon and then that's Alice and Ginnie over there, waving at those boys, the naughty girls. Sorry! We're such a big family now that it's a bit hard for anyone to take in,' said Mum, because Mrs Mann was looking so stunned.

The horses started to edge forwards very very slowly, u-u-u-u-p and d-o-w-n. My tummy went up and down too as Mrs Mann looked at me.

'So you're part of a very big family, Laura?' she said.

'Yes, Mrs Mann,' I said, in a very small voice.

'Well, you do surprise me,' she said.

'Nana, Nana!' said Rosie, taking hold of Mrs Mann's nose and wiggling it backwards and forwards affectionately. Mrs Mann simply chuckled. I wondered how she'd react if any of our class tweaked her nose!

'We seem to be surprising each other,' shouted Mrs Mann, as the music got louder and the roundabout revved up. 'Well, Laura, judging by your long and utterly convincing auto-biographical essay, you are obviously either a pathological liar – or a born writer. We'll give you the benefit of the doubt. You have the most vivid imagination of any child I've ever taught. You will obviously go far.'

And then the music was too loud for talking and the horses whirled round and round and round. I sat tight on my ostrich and it spread its crimson wings and we flew far over the fair, all the way up and over the moon.

THE END

So you think you know about

FAMiLY

in Jacqueline Wilson's books?

Ban your brothers from the room, ask your sisters for their help and test your memory of the books with these tough teasers. And if no one in the family can work it out, answers are at the back of the book.

1. What are Em's younger brother and sister called in *Clean Break*?

2. In whose house do Em and her family live?

3. Where does Floss's mum move to in *Candyfloss*?

4. Who threatens to name her new baby stepsister Ethel?

5. Where did Andy and her parents use to live before she became *The Suitcase Kid*?

6. Who does Jasmine live with in *Midnight*?

7. How many siblings does Charlie have in *The Lottie Project*?

8. When Charlie makes her grandparents a cake, what are they celebrating?

9. What job does Gemma's grandpa do in *Best Friends*?

10. Who's the oldest sibling: Callum, Jack or Gemma?

11. What's Biscuits' family name?

12. Who is Pippa and Hank's joke-telling older sister?

13. How many younger brothers has Naomi got, in the bed-and-breakfast hotel?

14. Why is Marigold *The Illustrated Mum*?

15. Who does Dolphin manage to find, working in a swimming pool?

What's in a NAME?

Lots of us are fascinated by the meaning of given names – our own and others'.
Do we live up to the meaning of our name or is it irrelevant?
Could it ever have any influence over what we do?

What do you think the characters with these names would
make of their meanings? And do you think
Jacqueline had any particular intention in mind?

Andy (Andrea)
Womanly
Perhaps the Suitcase
Kid will grow up to be
ultra-slinky?!

Alice
Truth, nobility
Alice does usually try
to do the right thing –
despite Gemma's
daft ideas!

Charlie and Lottie (Charlotte)
Little woman, born to command
Not so little but definitely
born to be in charge, thinks
Charlie, even if her Victorian
namesake wasn't.

Cam (Camilla)
Noble and righteous
Tracy doesn't always feel that
Cam lives up to this meaning, but
even Tracy admits that she'd try
anyone's patience!

Elsa *Oath of God*
Elsa hears quite a lot of oaths
from Mack the Smack, but they
don't exactly sound godly!
Anyway, her mum named her after a
lioness who featured in a famous old
book and film, because she had
a mane of hair when
she was born.

Em (Emily)
Industrious
Em certainly works jolly hard keeping
Vita and Maxie entertained but
prefers the more glamorous
meaning of Dad's nickname
for her – Emerald.

82

Jasmine
Fragrant flower
Exotic Jasmine is perfectly named as far as her friend Violet is concerned.

Gemma
Precious stone
Although she sometimes drives her mum mad, the whole family, and of course her best friend Alice, agree she's a real gem!

Garnet
Red gemstone
Garnet is perfectly happy to be named after a gemstone, just like her mother Opal was.

Sadie *Princess*
With a mum who's a childminder and a house full of demanding babies and toddlers, Sadie's lifestyle isn't very royal but her mum really appreciates her help and definitely thinks she's a princess.

Ruby
Precious red jewel
Ruby can't help reminding her identical twin sister that rubies are more precious than garnets – but she knows it doesn't really matter.

Violet
Modest flower
Violet can't help feeling it's right that she's named after a modest flower – she wouldn't feel right being named after a big, bright, bold one.

Tracy *Summer/battler /path*
Appropriately enough, there are as many different definitions of this name as Tracy Beaker has moods. She's certainly a battler, often on the warpath but can be as pleasant as a summer day – when she wants to be!

Verity *Truth*
It can be a bit of a burden knowing your name means 'truth' when you're trying to conceal a dead cat wrapped in sheets and lavender bath salts at the back of your wardrobe . . .

Vicky (Victoria)
The victorious one
Yup, that's Vicky Angel, always the winner of every argument.

Jacky's Childhood Photo Gallery

Jacky was born on 17th December 1915 and grew up to have a very vivid imagination. Read more about her childhood in her autobiography, *Jacky Daydream*.

Jacky with her mum Biddy and her dad Harry

Jacky as a baby

Jacky and her dolls

Jacky's first home

Off to school

On holiday
in Clacton

Mother and daughter

School photo: Jacky is in
the third row, on the left

Just Jacky

Her friends

Jacky with Alan,
her first boyfriend

Father and daughter

Drawing for Jacqueline

You might think Nick has a dream job, drawing pictures for a living. It is a great job, but it's harder work than you might imagine.

When Nick drew Floss for *Candyfloss* he did lots of rough drawings first to get her face and fluffy hair just right.

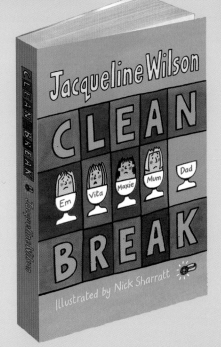

Nick tries out various ideas and colour
schemes before deciding on the final cover.
He uses special colour charts to help him.

Here's how Nick created an illustration for *Starring Tracy Beaker*.

Nick does his first rough drawings in a soft pencil. He works on layout paper which is very thin paper that he can use to trace over the previous rough, improving things and adding details. He uses a technical pen for his later roughs and for the final artwork, and nowadays he usually adds tone on a computer.

How to make Jacqueline's Favourite Fruity Refreshment

A smoothie is a delicious fruity, thick drink that is ultra-yummy but also mega-healthy. It's a brilliant drink after school when you need something tasty and energy-filled but Mum's begging you not to fill up before supper. It's also perfect after swimming or gym or for a late breakfast treat at the weekend. Em would love one when she's been to the Early Bird swimming sessions, Charlie could make a strawberry one for her red bedroom picnic and Tracy would choose the biggest, thickest one ever.

1 Choose a fruit to be the base of the smoothie. Bananas work particularly well as they make a thick, smooth mixture when put through a blender. It's great to combine a couple of different fruits — see what's going spare in the kitchen. Berries of any type are delicious and the more different types you use, the better the mixture of vitamins and goodies you're packing in. Smoothies are a perfect way of using up any fruit that's too ripe to last another day! Try strawberries, blueberries, mangoes, kiwi fruit — whatever's available.

2 Pick something to thicken your smoothie. Ice cream adds a luxurious touch but yoghurt is really delicious and healthier. Why not try frozen yoghurt for a summer treat?

Here's how to do it:

YOGHURT

3 You'll need to add enough liquid to make sure everything blends smoothly. Try a little milk or soya drink or fruit juice. Add more if needed.

MILK

4 Finally, put everything into a blender and mix till smooth. Then refrigerate or pour into glasses and serve immediately.

Enjoy!

What Happened Next?

When we asked you to come up with a continuation of the story in any one of Jacqueline Wilson's books, the website was flooded with replies. It seems hundreds of you are budding writers bursting with ideas to extend the lives of your favourite characters. From the strikingly unusual to the reassuringly familiar and from the frightening to the hilarious, you had dozens of bright ideas and well-written endings for us to choose from. Jacqueline loved reading your entries and was delighted at how brilliantly you'd taken over her characters and added to their stories. Below are the three entries which Jacqueline judged to be the best for the originality of their plots and their faithfulness to the original characters.

A new ending for **The Diamond Girls**
by Emma Halligan, 11, from Coventry

Martine did have a girl, in the end. Mum came up with loads and loads of names for the baby, but Martine settled for a nice, popular name, Lily. Lily's inherited Martine's looks, Mum's thick, black hair, Jude's boyish nature, Rochelle's cuteness, and my eyes. We still live in Mercury, but there is no Mary to keep me company any more. She was sent to a foster home a few weeks ago. I miss her, but I have loads of other friends now. They heard about me and what I did with Mary and were immediately clamouring to be my friend. Bruce lives with us now. He helps out with Sundance and Lily and plays with me and Bluebell. He buys Rochelle make-up and hair clips, teaches Jude all sorts of different martial arts and he is always willing to lend Martine a bit of cash when she's running out. My plaster cast came off a few weeks ago now, and my leg is fine again, if not a little bit tender . . . but I can't look across the street without seeing that chilling vision of Mary jumping out of the window . . .

A new ending for **Lola Rose**
by Imogen Abbot, 15, from London

Dear Diary,

The first thing you should know is that I'm not the sort of person to write in a diary, but my social worker thinks it will help me 'find my inner self and let out my feelings'! Everything went totally freaky after Mum — I can't say it — after Mum went away. The cancer came back and she couldn't fight it off. For a while I stopped speaking, sleeping, and eating, but I'm over that now. Of course I still miss her, and so does Kendall but we had to pull through.

So Kenny got to go back to Auntie Barbara, because he was little. But I'm too old and 'problematic', so I ended up in care with Elaine as my social worker. I was so mad that I got stuck here in this dump, I had to spend a lot of time in the quiet room trying to calm down. One of the worst things is that I can't see Harpreet any more. We do write letters but I can never get a chance on the computer because there's only one for the whole dumping ground. I also had to stop being Lola Rose Luck because it wasn't on my birth certificate. I'm Jayni again now.

Dear Diary,

I was supposed to be seeing Kenny and Barbara today, but I can't go now because Elaine is dealing with a new teenage girl who is moving here, a girl called Tanya who got kicked out of her foster home for shoplifting. She's much older than us but is supposedly good with little kids. I'm kind of scared of her because she's really tough, with bright orange hair sticking right up in the air.

I've just had dinner, and it turns out that Tanya is really nice. We got chatting halfway up the stairs and it seems like we both fell out of the same boat, leaving younger siblings behind. Tanya said she liked to play with people's hair so I let her do mine — she styled it for me in this twisty thing on top. She said she'd had lots of practice doing that hairstyle on her neighbour. So I suppose we're friends now. Maybe things mightn't be quite so bad if I've got a friend?

There's another ray of light too! Elaine told me today that one of the girls who used to be in this dumping ground recently got fostered off to a single woman, but she keeps getting into fights and bunking off school. They think she needs someone to guide her the right way and the woman is interested in fostering a sensible girl to help her little tearaway. I really want to live with Auntie Barbara and Kendall, but as that's not possible, maybe a nice foster mum wouldn't be so bad? Hopefully I can still see Tanya . . .

A new ending for **Midnight**
by Ryan Woods, 16, from Norfolk

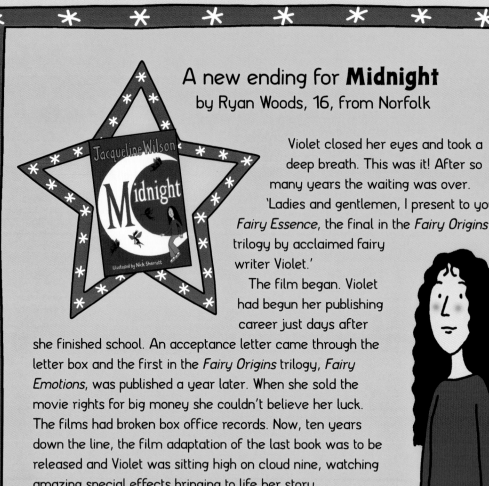

Violet closed her eyes and took a deep breath. This was it! After so many years the waiting was over.

'Ladies and gentlemen, I present to you, *Fairy Essence*, the final in the *Fairy Origins* trilogy by acclaimed fairy writer Violet.'

The film began. Violet had begun her publishing career just days after she finished school. An acceptance letter came through the letter box and the first in the *Fairy Origins* trilogy, *Fairy Emotions*, was published a year later. When she sold the movie rights for big money she couldn't believe her luck. The films had broken box office records. Now, ten years down the line, the film adaptation of the last book was to be released and Violet was sitting high on cloud nine, watching amazing special effects bringing to life her story.

As the final credits disappeared, a roar of approval swept the room. Violet blushed. Her dream had been achieved and she knew there was still so much more to come.

'Thank you' she said, a tear forming in the corner of her eye. '*Fairy Origins* has been a journey of nearly fifteen years now . . . What a journey!'

Jacky FACT

Jacqueline has met the Queen at Buckingham Palace

Jacqueline talks about 'What happens next . . .'

Children frequently write to me asking me what happens next in my books. This is a brilliant game. I love playing it myself but I don't always know the answers. When I've finished a book the characters wave goodbye and then run off, leaving me behind. They rarely get in touch with me to tell me what they've been doing.

Just occasionally a favourite character lurks in a corner of my mind, giving me a little nudge every now and then. Tracy Beaker never wants to go away! She likes being the centre of my attention and hates it when I write about anyone else.

I was quite happy to keep her just in one book, *The Story of Tracy Beaker*, but she had other ideas.

She kept saying, 'What about me? Let's find out if I live happily ever after.'

So many real children wrote begging me to start a new book about Tracy that I gave in.

What about me?

95

I had great fun writing *The Dare Game* and it seemed to please everyone so I thought, Hurray, that's it, I'm done with Little Ms Bossy-Boots Beaker. But then the television series started, and then there was the partwork magazine, and the stage play — not to mention all the Tracy Beaker notebooks and pens and bags and pyjamas and knickers . . .

Tracy was always on my mind, so I decided to write one more story about her, *Starring Tracy Beaker*, where Tracy gets to be the star of her school play at Christmas. I think I'm done with her now, but you never know with Tracy. I might find myself writing *Tracy Teenager*, *Tracy Falls in Love*, *Tracy Beaker's Baby*, *Tracy Beaker Career Girl*, *Tracy Beaker's Mid-Life Crisis* . . .

Biscuits crops up in three books now, mostly because I'm so fond of him. My mouth always waters when I write his scenes because we're both pretty greedy! I loved the sound of all Biscuits' cakes in *Best Friends*. I've also deliberately written my four *Girls* books as a series. I've had lots of requests for yet another book about Ellie, Magda and Nadine, but I've no plans for a new one at the moment, though they might one day make a guest appearance in someone else's book.

If I were to write a sequel to any of my other books, it might well be *The Diamond Girls*, because I'd like to know if the five sisters are doing OK. Goodness knows what they've all been up to. I think all sorts of dramas will always happen to that family, but they've got a knack of being happy in spite of everything.

I'm not so sure about Dolphin and Star and Marigold in *The Illustrated Mum*. This is probably my favourite out of my books, and I so hope Marigold recovers and is able to cope and look after the girls again. She'll certainly try . . .

I feel less worried about Lola Rose and Kendall in *Lola Rose*. I hope that their mum gets completely better, and that they all live at the pub with Auntie Barbara. She'll look after them all, no problem!

I've often wondered whether Mandy and Tanya in *Bad Girls* ever get together again. It will be hard for them to stay in touch, but I feel their friendship means so much to both of them that they'll try their hardest. I was once asked to write the script for a film of *Bad Girls* and I changed things so that Mandy and Tanya run away together. Maybe one day I'll write this part as a proper sequel.

I don't yet know in detail what will happen to any of them. But there's one sequel I know all about. I've written *Jacky Daydream* about my childhood, from the day I was born to the summer I was eleven. I think one day I'll definitely write a sequel about my teenage years and how I got started as a writer.

Jacky FACT

Jacqueline's favourite place to go on holiday is Boston in America

How to dress like Jacqueline Wilson

I never really liked the way I looked as a child. I wanted to grow my hair and have plaits or a ponytail, but my mum said my hair was too untidy and wispy. She always made me have it chopped off short. My mum had very definite ideas about my clothes too. When I was little I loved fancy flouncy dresses with flared skirts and petticoats but my mum didn't go for this look at all.

My dresses were nearly always plain and boring. There was one frock I particularly hated that was grey!

Things didn't improve when I was a teenager. I longed to look cool. I still wanted long hair, but now I wanted it hanging loose to my waist, with a heavy fringe in front. I longed for jewellery, especially silver bangles and big rings. I was no longer a girl for frills and flounces. I wanted to wear a big black sweater and a short black skirt and black tights and black pointy boots. Fat chance! I started to grow my hair but it got stuck in that awful straggly in between stage so that I lost patience and had it cut even shorter. I had a Saturday job when I was fifteen but I didn't earn enough to buy jewellery or my own clothes. My mum didn't like jewellery on young girls, but she bought me a little pearl necklace for my birthday – sadly not my sort of jewellery at all. She bought old-fashioned

pastel clothes for me because she wanted me to look ladylike.

It's so lovely to be grown up and able to wear things that I like! My hair is shorter than ever but I've got used to it now. It's turned silver, but it matches all my beautiful big silver rings and bangles. I get them from this fantastic shop in London called the Great Frog. I wear black clothes nearly all the time too. I think I'll still be wearing black with lots of silver jewellery when I'm an ancient old lady. Maybe I'll have a black walking stick embossed with silver!

If you fancy dressing like me then simply wear any kind of black clothes, especially anything with a black lace trim or black velvet. Black tights are essential, and funky black shoes or boots. You'll probably have to wait till you're grown up for wonderful Great Frog jewellery, but you can wear lots of pretty Indian bangles and cheap glass rings. Don't chop your hair off in a spiky J.W. style though – that's going too far!

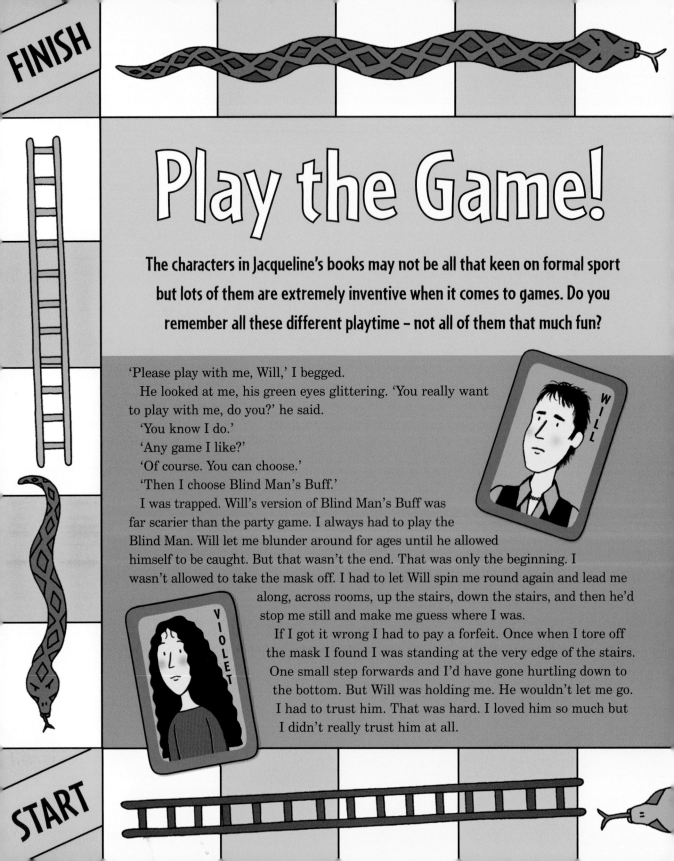

Play the Game!

The characters in Jacqueline's books may not be all that keen on formal sport but lots of them are extremely inventive when it comes to games. Do you remember all these different playtime – not all of them that much fun?

'Please play with me, Will,' I begged.

He looked at me, his green eyes glittering. 'You really want to play with me, do you?' he said.

'You know I do.'

'Any game I like?'

'Of course. You can choose.'

'Then I choose Blind Man's Buff.'

I was trapped. Will's version of Blind Man's Buff was far scarier than the party game. I always had to play the Blind Man. Will let me blunder around for ages until he allowed himself to be caught. But that wasn't the end. That was only the beginning. I wasn't allowed to take the mask off. I had to let Will spin me round again and lead me along, across rooms, up the stairs, down the stairs, and then he'd stop me still and make me guess where I was.

If I got it wrong I had to pay a forfeit. Once when I tore off the mask I found I was standing at the very edge of the stairs. One small step forwards and I'd have gone hurtling down to the bottom. But Will was holding me. He wouldn't let me go. I had to trust him. That was hard. I loved him so much but I didn't really trust him at all.

FINISH

START

'Tim?' said Jake. 'Open your eyes! Now, your pal Biscuits is down there waiting for you. Come on Start backing towards the edge.'

I backed one step. Then another. Then I stopped.

'I can't!'

'Yes you can,' said Jake. 'You'll see. Over you go. Don't worry. You can't fall. You just have to remember, you don't let go of the rope.'

I started at him and started backing some more. Then my heels suddenly lost contact with the ground. I slipped backwards and suddenly . . . there I was! Suspended. In mid-air.

'Help!'

I reached forward, desperate.

I had to hang on to something.

I grabbed at the rock.

I let go of the rope!

'Why don't you play party games?'

'Party games? Like what?' I said.

'Like, boring,' said Chloe.

'No, no, they're good fun,' Dad insisted. 'Let's all go indoors and play.'

When Chloe turned to go Dad mimed hitting her over the head with his wooden mallet. Emily and Amy and Bella and I all fell about laughing.

'What's so funny?' said Chloe crossly.

'Nothing. We're just having fun,' I said.

And we did have fun. Dad showed us how to play all these weird old-fashioned party games like Squeak Piggy Squeak. When Chloe was the pig she sat on my lap so hard I squeaked for real but I didn't care.

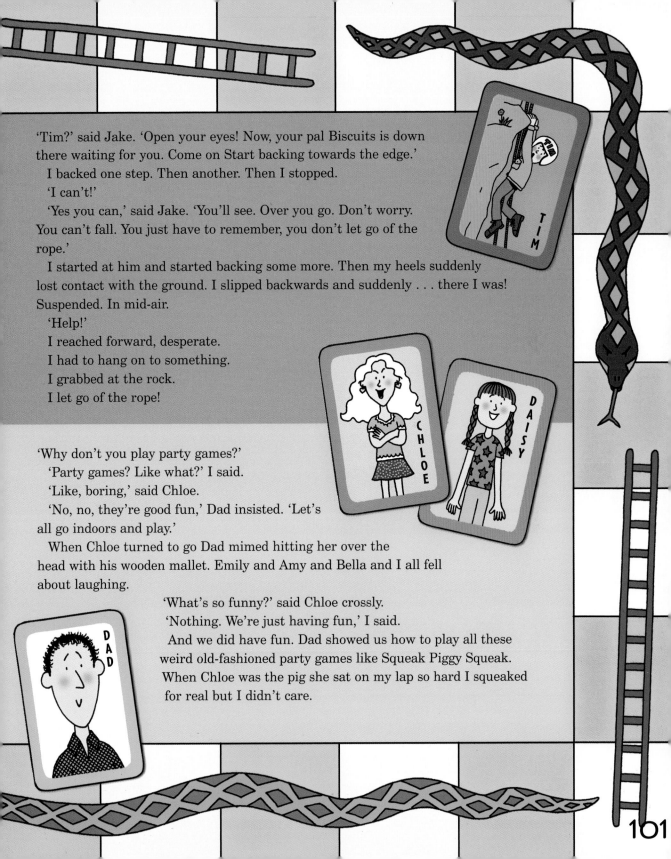

I thought hard. 'OK. You get to dare me now.'

'I don't really want to, thank you.'

I couldn't believe his attitude. Didn't he realize the potential of my offer??? 'Go on, Alexander,' I said impatiently, standing over him.

Alexander wriggled backwards on his bony bottom. 'I can't make up any dares,' he said meekly. 'You make one up, Tracy.'

'Don't be so wet! Come on. Dare me to do something really really wicked.'

Alexander thought hard. Then I saw light in his pale blue eyes. 'All right. I dare you to . . . I dare you to . . . stand on your head.'

He just didn't get it! But I decided to show willing. I spat on my hands and sprang forward. 'Easy-peasy,' I said, upside down.

'Gosh! You're really good at it.'

'Anyone can stand on their head.'

'I can't.'

I might have known. I tried hard to show him. He was useless. He just crumpled in a heap whenever he tried to kick his legs up.

'Watch me!' I said, doing headstands and handstands and then a cartwheel round the room.

'I can see your knickers,' said Alexander, giggling.

'Well, don't look,' I said breathlessly.

'I can't help it,' said Alexander. Then he started singing this weird song about leaping up and down and waving your knickers in the air.

'You what?' I said, right way up again.

'It's a song,' said Alexander. 'My dad sings it when he's in a good mood. Which isn't often when I'm around.' He sang it again.

'Is that another dare?' I said.

Alexander giggled.

'Right!' I said, and I whipped my knickers off and leapt up and down waving them like a flag.

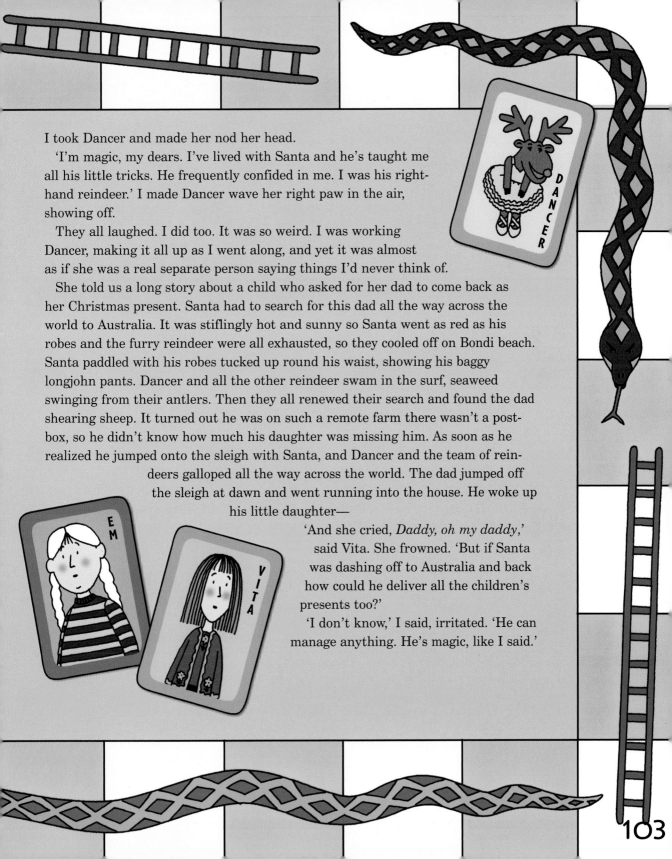

I took Dancer and made her nod her head.

'I'm magic, my dears. I've lived with Santa and he's taught me all his little tricks. He frequently confided in me. I was his right-hand reindeer.' I made Dancer wave her right paw in the air, showing off.

They all laughed. I did too. It was so weird. I was working Dancer, making it all up as I went along, and yet it was almost as if she was a real separate person saying things I'd never think of.

She told us a long story about a child who asked for her dad to come back as her Christmas present. Santa had to search for this dad all the way across the world to Australia. It was stiflingly hot and sunny so Santa went as red as his robes and the furry reindeer were all exhausted, so they cooled off on Bondi beach. Santa paddled with his robes tucked up round his waist, showing his baggy longjohn pants. Dancer and all the other reindeer swam in the surf, seaweed swinging from their antlers. Then they all renewed their search and found the dad shearing sheep. It turned out he was on such a remote farm there wasn't a post-box, so he didn't know how much his daughter was missing him. As soon as he realized he jumped onto the sleigh with Santa, and Dancer and the team of rein-deers galloped all the way across the world. The dad jumped off the sleigh at dawn and went running into the house. He woke up his little daughter—

'And she cried, *Daddy, oh my daddy,*' said Vita. She frowned. 'But if Santa was dashing off to Australia and back how could he deliver all the children's presents too?'

'I don't know,' I said, irritated. 'He can manage anything. He's magic, like I said.'

Jacqueline's BEST Films

My favourite film when I was a little girl was called *Mandy*. I don't think it's available on DVD but every now and then they show it on afternoon television. It's a 1950s black and white film and people talk in that clipped, very proper way that sounds silly nowadays – but it still grips me and moves me to tears. It's about a little deaf girl called Mandy who's five or six. She's played by the child actress Mandy Miller. I thought she was wonderful and went to every film she made subsequently and kept a big scrapbook of photos and cuttings about her.

She gave the most touching performance as the little deaf child, with her big dark eyes and sad expression. Her parents are always having terrible arguments because they have different ideas about how Mandy should be brought up. Her father wants to hide her away at home with a private teacher. Her mother wants her to go to a boarding school for deaf children where they will be able to teach her properly. Mandy goes to the school but she's terribly unhappy and lonely at first. You see her crying at night, unable to understand why she's been sent away. Mandy's mother becomes very friendly with the gruff but brilliant headteacher and this causes more problems – but eventually everything is sorted out and Mandy has learned to say a few words and has made friends with other children. Do try and watch it if you can. I promise it's really, really good!

My daughter Emma's favourite film when she was small was *Picnic at Hanging Rock*, a visually stunning Australian film about girls in a turn-of-the-century boarding school. They go on a special picnic on Valentine's Day and climb the great hanging rock and then three girls mysteriously go missing. You never really find out what happened to them, which irritated me no end, but Emma didn't seem to mind. She watched the film until she could chant it by heart, particularly entranced by blonde and beautiful Miranda in her cream lace dress. I preferred sad, dark, orphaned Sarah who dramatically kills herself by leaping out of the window and crashing through the greenhouse roof. *Picnic at Hanging Rock* isn't really a suitable film for children!

I've been thrilled with the television film adaptations of my own books. Long ago there was a schools television version of *Cliffhanger*, and later a stylish *Double Act* with identical twins Chloe and Zoe playing Ruby and Garnet. There was a very funny film of *Best Friends*, a colourful version of *Girls in Love*, and many fantastic episodes of *The Story of Tracy Beaker*, including a spin-off film *The Movie of Me*. I think my all time favourite adaptation has been *The Illustrated Mum*. The girls playing Dolphin and Star gave very moving performances and Michelle Collins as Marigold was brilliant. Cilla Ware directed The Illustrated Mum with great flair and imagination. It won an American Emmy and had a very special showing at the Museum of Modern Art in New York.

How to make a scrapbook

India and Treasure have their diaries, Tracy Beaker writes 'My Book About Me', and of course Charlie has her Lottie Project, but for a really fabulous way to record and remember all your special moments, have you ever thought about making a scrapbook? It's easy, great fun and you end up with a beautiful book that's completely unique and precious to you.

Start off with a large-format album of empty pages – it doesn't have to be fancy or expensive. Don't worry about the cover for now – it's best to personalize it yourself anyway.

Decide whether you want a specific theme for your scrapbook or whether it's going to be a general record of your life and interests. If you want to concentrate on one theme, are you going to make a scrapbook about a particular event (e.g. being a bridesmaid or going on a camping holiday) or a particular interest (e.g. cats or ballet or books)?

leaf from special walk

Start saving special things to stick in your scrapbook. Anything that can be stuck or mounted on a page can be included. Postcards and photographs look great. You can cut out pictures from magazines (just like Lola Rose does). Save tickets or theatre programmes, brochures and flyers. Scraps of fabric, feathers, ribbons, badges, locks of hair, cards, leaves, pressed flowers, drawings are perfect – if it reminds you of something important, happy or special, stick it in.

holiday snap

Keep an eye open for papers or cards with interesting or unusual patterns, colours or textures, and bits of newspaper or magazines with unusual fonts or photos. If you get really into it, you can also buy lots of specialist bits and bobs in craft shops, newsagents or on-line through specialist scrapbooking websites.

Get yourself going by doing just one page layout from start to finish. Once you've picked your theme for the album, choose just a handful of photos or mementoes to include on a page, e.g. three photos and a ticket.

Pick a shape or colour design to unify your page – use lots of circles or keep all decorations in shades of green and white, for example.

my favourite author

ROXY CINEMA
B36 ADMITS ONE
224530

Do you want to mount the photos or other things on coloured or patterned paper to give them a more interesting background? Or decorate around them with glitter, beads or ribbon strips?

Think about cropping the photos to fit more on the page. You can cut them into circles, heart shapes, crop corners with zig-zag scissors etc.

TOFFEE WHIRL

Add some **words** to tell you what the page is all about. You may think it's obvious **who's who** and **when** and **where** it all happened, but will you still **remember** it in a few years' time or when you're **grown up?**

Once you've done your first page, you're on your way! Just keep going. Do it as often or as infrequently as you like – it shouldn't be a chore. Keep your eyes open, have fun and be creative!

Get Tracy Beaker's Attitude!

Want to talk the talk and walk the walk, just like Tracy? Here's Tracy's Top Ten Tips on how to do it:

I am completely brilliant!

1 Remember: tough kids don't cry! (But an occasional attack of hay fever can't be helped.)

2 Make sure that you tell everyone that you are completely brilliant and the best child ever!

3 If you get offered a piece of cake, ask for the whole thing. It's worth a try — and it might even work.

4 If there's something you want, just keep on hinting . . . and hinting . . . and hinting . . . and asking outright!

Fast car

5 Never ever let anyone beat you at the Dare Game — be sure to think of something even tougher and trickier for them to do next.

6 Be careful who you make friends with — beware of anyone who might reveal your most private secrets.

7 Don't leave your football where anyone else can find it.

8 If your sheets sometimes mysteriously get extremely damp in the middle of the night, make sure you know where the clean, dry ones are kept.

9 Share the greatness! Give your friends and family the benefit of your superior wisdom.

10 When in doubt — go for it!

109

Whose Home?

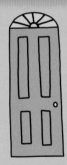

Although nearly all Jacqueline's characters live in houses or flats in towns there's still a great variety in their homes. Do you remember who lives in these places?

A white cottage with a grey slate roof and a black chimney and a bright butter-yellow front door. There were yellow roses and honeysuckle growing up a lattice round the door and the leaded windows, and lots of other flowers growing in the big garden. In the middle of the garden was an old twisted tree with big branches bent almost to the ground. Mum and Dad were so taken by the cottage that they'd stopped keeping an eye on me. I toddled through the gate and made for the tree because it was studded all over with soft dark fruit. I picked a berry and popped it in my mouth. It tasted sweet and sharp and sensational. My very first mulberry.

There was a For Sale notice on the fence. It seemed like we were meant to buy Mulberry Cottage. It wasn't quite in the country. It turned out to have a lot of dry rot and woodworm and for the first year there was dust everywhere and we couldn't use half the rooms. But it didn't matter. We'd found our fairy-tale cottage.

I've got my own bedroom but it's not a patch on my room at the Children's Home. It's not much bigger than a cupboard. Cam's so mean too. She said I could choose to have my bedroom exactly the way I wanted. Well, I had some great ideas. I wanted a king-size bed with a white satin duvet and my own dressing table with lights all round the mirror like a film star and white carpet as soft and thick as cat fur and my own computer to write my stories on and my own sound system and a giant white television and video and a trapeze hanging from the ceiling so I could practise circus tricks and my own ensuite bathroom so I could splash all day in my own private bubble bath.

Cam acted like I was joking. When she realized I wasn't joining in the general laughter she said, 'Come on, Trace, how could all that stuff ever fit in the box room?'

Yeah, quite. Why should I be stuck in the box room? Am I a box? Why can't I have Cam's room? I mean, she's got hardly any stuff, just a lot of books and a little bed. She could easily fit in the box room.

I did my best to persuade her. I wheedled and whined for all I was worth – but she didn't budge. So I ended up in this little rubbish room and I'm supposed to think it a huge big deal because I was allowed to choose the colour paint and pick a new duvet cover and curtains. I chose black to match my mood.

I didn't think Cam would take me seriously but she gave in on that one. Black walls. Black ceiling. She suggested luminous silver stars which are kind of a good idea. I'm not too keen on the dark. I'm not scared. I'm not scared of anything. But I like to look up from my bed and see those stars glowing up above.

There were a few ex-council flats we could have managed, posher than the Newborough Estate, but Jo wasn't having that.

'We want something private,' she said. 'Small but select.'

And that's what we've got. A one-bedroomed flat in a quiet block with laid-out gardens. No one tore out the roses or smashed the windows or peed in the lift. The people living there were mostly elderly ladies or young married couples or schoolteachers who don't usually tear and smash and pee publicly. They looked a bit nervously at Jo and me when we moved in – especially me – but Jo insisted we had to be on our Best Behaviour at all times.

There is nothing for it. I have to leave home.

I love my home very much, although it is only a tumbledown cottage, stifling hot in the summer and bitter cold in winter. The winters have always been the worst. Two little brothers and one infant sister died during the winter months, and Father passed away last February when the snow was thick on the ground.

I did not cry when Father died. Perhaps it is wicked to admit this, but I felt relieved. He treated Mother very bad, and though he earned a fair wage he drank a great deal of it. So we were always poor even then, but Mother kept our simple home shining bright. She made bright rag rugs to cover the cold stone flags of the floor and each bed upstairs had a pretty patchwork quilt. I cut out pictures from the illustrated papers and pinned them to the walls. I even pinned pictures out in the privy!

There was always a rabbit stew bubbling on the black-leaded range when we came home from school. We'd dig potatoes or carrots or cabbage from the garden, and in the summer Rose and Jessie and I would pick a big bunch of flowers to go in the pink jug Frank won at the fair.

We were meant to be looking for our own place in Scotland but we never found one. Then my sister Pippa got born and Mack fell out with his pal and lost his job. Mum got ever so worried. She didn't get on very well with my sort-of gran and it got worse after Pippa was born.

So we moved back down South and said we were homeless. Mum got even more worried. She thought we'd be put in a bed-and-breakfast hotel. She said she'd never live it down. (Little did she know. You don't have to live it down. You can live it up.)

But we didn't get put in a bed-and-breakfast hotel then. We were offered this flat on a big estate. It was a bit grotty but Mack said he'd fix it up so it would look like a palace. So we moved in. It was a pretty weirdo palace, if you ask me. There was green mould on the walls and creepy-crawlies in the kitchen. Mack tried slapping a bit of paint about but it didn't make much difference. Mum got ever so depressed and Mack got cross. Pippa kept getting coughs and colds and snuffling, because of the damp.

I was OK though. My campbed collapsed once and for all, so I got to have a new bed.

So you think you know about

CLOTHES

in Jacqueline Wilson's books?

Unzip your boots, curl up in your cosiest cardie and have a go at these stylish posers! Answers are revealed at the back of the book.

 1 What items of clothing does Kim taunt Mandy for wearing at the beginning of *Bad Girls*?

 2 What does Gemma's mum make her wear for Alice's leaving party in *Best Friends*?

 3 What outfit does Gemma ask for as her birthday present?

 4 What does Dolphin in *The Illustrated Mum* usually wear for school?

 5 What are Ruby and Garnet pictured wearing on the cover of *Double Act*?

6 What does Treasure's nan wear for her line-dancing classes in *Secrets*?

7 What does Dad buy Gran for Christmas in *Clean Break*?

8 What does Em wear as a top when Dad takes them out on New Year's Day?

9 What does Violet first notice about Jasmine when she joins the class as a new girl, in *Midnight*?

10 What special hat does Gemma's mum let Sadie try on in *The Mum-minder*?

11 What does Tim's mum buy him for his activity holiday in *Cliffhanger*?

12 What clothes does Tracy Beaker's mum give her for her birthday in *The Dare Game*?

13 What does Daisy consider wearing for Amy's party but is glad she hasn't?

14 And what does she actually wear?

Hunt the Baby

A Story by Jacqueline Wilson

Who's there?

Boo.

Boo who?

No need to cry, it's only a joke!

I'm Elsa. I'm always telling jokes. I drive everyone daft.

I live in the Star Hotel. It's ever so posh. Don't get the wrong idea. We're not rich. We're so poor we lost our house and had to live crowded into one room in this truly crummy hotel, but then there was a fire (I raised the alarm and got to be so famous I was on television!) so for the moment we've been re-housed. Well, re-hoteled.

In the Star Hotel we feel like stars and we all go twinkle-twinkle. Even my stepdad Mack. He hasn't smacked me once since we've been here. My mum doesn't go to bed during the day any more. My little sister Pippa hasn't wet the bed once. But my baby brother Hank hasn't half caused a lot of trouble!

Hank doesn't cry much. He eats heaps. He goes to sleep straight away when you tuck him up in his bed. By the way, what animal goes to sleep with its shoes on? A horse! Hank goes to sleep in his bed, yes. But he doesn't stay there. You can tuck him up really tight so he can hardly turn over and then you can cage him in – and yet when you wake up in the morning and look in his bed – he's gone! You have to play Hunt Little Hank: under our beds, in the bathroom, in the wardrobe. Once he got right out of the door and down the corridor before we caught up with him. He can't even walk yet, but he's a champion crawler.

He's never been properly lost though – until the Sunday we went to this car boot sale. Hey, what birds hover over people lost in the dessert? Luncheon vultures!

It was a really super-duper sale, with ice-cream vans and sweet stalls and a round-about for little kids and heaps of people selling clothes and videos and T-shirts and toys. Mum spotted this fantastic sparkly top and started trying it on. She told us to watch Hank. Mack took Pippa off to get ice cream. Aha – what did the baby ghost say when he wanted his favourite food? I scream! I dashed after Mack to make sure mine had a chocolate flake and then I turned back to Hank in his buggy and – you've guessed it. He'd slipped his reins and scampered.

I searched everywhere. No Hank. Mum ran round calling him, stopping everyone to see if they'd seen a baby boy. Nobody had. We started to panic. Mack and Pippa came back with the ice creams and Mack got mega-miffed with me and I thought maybe I was going to get smacked after all. No-one felt like eating their ice creams and they trickled down Mack's arms. My tears were trickling too because it looked like Hank was really lost this time.

I tried hard to work out where in the world he'd got to. Where would he make for? Had he wanted an ice cream? What about sweets from a stall? I whirled round, trying to spot him. Round and round about. Hey! The roundabout!

I was right! Hank was sitting up straight in this little toy train on the roundabout, grinning and gurgling gleefully. 'He must have climbed up all by himself,' said the man in charge of the roundabout. 'Well, he might as well have a good ride now he's here.'

We were so happy to have found him we all had a ride. Mum climbed in the train with Hank and hugged him hard even though she told him how bad he was to run – well, crawl – away. Mack clambered onto a big pink elephant with Pippa on his lap. How do you get down off an elephant? You can't. You get it off a swan.

I sat on a horse with a golden mane and played cowboys. Maybe I'll have to learn how to use a lasso sometime. Now that might be a great way of capturing my bad baby brother Hank if he makes another escape attempt: OK, one last joke. Why did the cowboy get into trouble? Because he couldn't stop horsing around. That's me, all right!

THE END

Nick's Sketch Pad

Tracy Beaker is my favourite character to illustrate.

I draw her arms just long enough to reach the tops of her legs.

I add tone to black and white pictures with diagonal lines (or little dots if I'm feeling patient!).

The way I draw Tracy's mouth and eyebrows gives her expression.

Sometimes she's happy, Sometimes she's sad. Sometimes she doesn't know how she feels!

When I draw a character I start with a pencil pin man.

I build up the figure and when I'm happy with it I trace out my final drawing in ink.

118

I draw the thumb lower down than the fingers

and I don't usually bother with nails.

People usually tuck in one hand when they fold their arms.

In a really deep frown the eyes and eyebrows meet.

My glamorous ladies can be quite curvy!

Superheroes need confident poses.

My old people often stoop.

My profiles work best when I draw the ear on the back of the head!

My babies have big heads and no necks.

Patterns add interest.

These are my favourite animals to illustrate.

These are all things I've found it useful to know how to draw. It's funny how often they crop up in my work!

Jacqueline at Nine

The Maggotts isn't a very long novel – it's only about twenty pages. It's rather like a baby version of one of my novels now. The Maggott family have more than their fair share of problems but they have a lot of fun too.

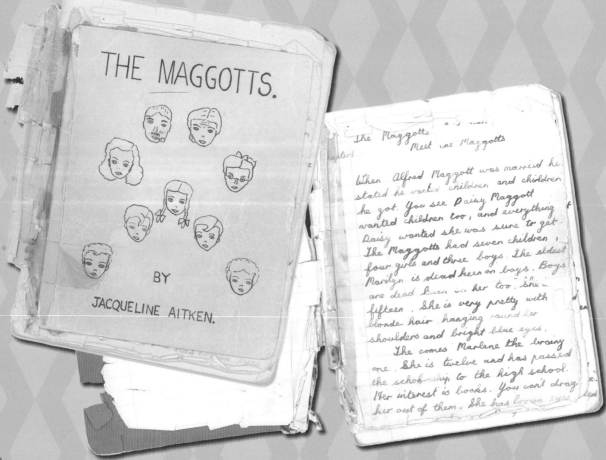

THE MAGGOTTS.

BY

JACQUELINE AITKEN.

The Maggotts

Meet the Maggotts

When Alfred Maggott was married he stated he wanted children and children he got. You see Daisy Maggott wanted children too, and everything Daisy wanted she was sure to get. The Maggotts had seven children, four girls and three boys. The oldest Marilyn is dead keen on boys. Boys are dead keen on her too. She is fifteen. She is very pretty with blonde hair hanging round her shoulders and bright blue eyes.

Then comes Marlene the brainy one. She is twelve and has passed the scholarship to the high school. Her interest is books. You can't drag her out of them. She has brown eyes

Nick at Nine

This was a very important drawing for me. I got to hold it up in assembly in front of the whole school and it was pinned up on the hall wall. Even more exciting — the husband of one of my teachers saw it and asked me to do a picture for him if he paid me £5. That's when I decided I wanted to be a professional artist when I grow up.

Join the FREE online
Jacqueline Wilson Fan Club at

www.jacquelinewilson.co.uk

Jacqueline Wilson co.uk Message Board

Remember: All new forum topics and replies are added to the Message Board every day at 5p.m.

Page 1 of 7

Next page

Jacqueline Wilson

Jacqueline Wilson

Jacqueline's Book!

Hello Jacqueline!

There's loads of exciting new stuff for you - your own private diary, pages where you can share your love of Jacqueline's books, new games and activities plus all the fun from before. Take a look through your book by clicking on the tabs now!

Jacky Daydream
by Jacqueline Wilson

Everybody knows Tracy Beaker, Jacqueline Wilson's best-loved character. But what do they know about Jacqueline herself? In this fascinating book, discover. . .

. . . how Jacky played with paper dolls like April in .

. . . how she dealt with an unpredictable father like Prue in .

. . . how she sat entrance exams like Ruby in Double Act.

But most of all how Jacky loved reading and writing stories. Losing herself in a new world was the best possible way she could think of spending her time. From the very first story she wrote, , it was clear that this little girl had a very vivid imagination. But who would've guessed that she would grow up to be the mega-bestselling, award-winning Jacqueline Wilson!

Jacqueline Wilson takes a look back at her own childhood in this captivating story of friendships, loneliness, books, toys, parents and much more. She explores her early years with the same warmth and lightness of touch that imbues her novels and covers such difficult issues as her parents' extra-marital affairs with delicacy. With photographs and new illustrations by Nick Sharratt,

RRP £12.99 Hardback

← BACK

Jacqueline Wilson

Jacqueline's Diary

Ask Jacqueline

Hobbies

Watch Jacqueline

FAQs

50 Questions

Photo Gallery

Links

Biography

News & Events

Goodbye!

Do you recognize these final pictures?

1

2

3

4

5

I wonder if you know what you want to be when you grow up? Perhaps you think you'd like to be a writer. I knew I wanted to be a writer ever since I can remember. I started playing all sorts of imaginary games when I was very little, long before I could read. I made up elaborate fantasy lands where I played with all sorts of pretend people. I used to play this when I woke up early in the morning, when I went to bed at night, when I was having my tea, when I was dragged round the shops with my mum. I even played my pretend games when I was sitting on the lavatory, but one time my mum and dad listened outside the door and heard me muttering and fell about laughing. I felt terribly embarrassed and silly and learned to pretend silently inside my head after that!

I only had a few picture books and I couldn't always get my mum to read to me, so I'd look at the illustrations and make up my own stories. I'd take a book with me on the bus to the shops. I'd pore over the pictures and say my stories out loud. Everyone on the bus thought this little three-year-old was reading fluently already. My mum kept quiet and took pride in having an infant phenomenon!

It was wonderful when I could read properly. I'd go to the library every week and read my way right through the shelves, from Louisa M. Alcott to Laura Ingalls Wilder. I started writing my own stories too, just a few laboriously pencilled sentences at first, illustrated with stick people with huge heads like lollipops, but by the time I was eight or nine I was filling fat Woolworths exercise books with long involved stories.

I was an only child so I liked making up stories about great big families. That's the wonderful thing about writing. You don't have to write about yourself and your own circumstances (though of course you can if you want to). You're free to make up anything you want. I remember I wrote a long play about Moses in the Bible and a fantasy story about a man with too many toes on his feet! However, I mostly wrote realistic stories about children with problems, little versions of the stories I write now. It was always my dream to get one of my stories published. I never thought that one day I'd have nearly ninety books with my name on, including this very special book. I do hope you've enjoyed reading it.

Jacqueline Wilson
xxx

Answers to Quizzes

So you think you know about . . . friendship in Jacqueline Wilson's books? (page 28)

1. Amy, Bella, Chloe, Daisy and Emily
2. Tanya
3. Naomi
4. The ladies' toilet at the Royal Hotel
5. Kitty, because that's what India's heroine, Anne Frank, called her diary
6. Tim
7. Justine
8. Matching denim outfits
9. Alexander and Football
10. Greg
11. A cake she has made
12. Robin
13. Drama Club
14. Because Sophie has four kittens
15. Giles

So you think you know about . . . school in Jacqueline Wilson's books? (page 62)

1. Maths
2. They teach teachers how to teach
3. Margot and Judy
4. Blob
5. The Victorians
6. *Romeo and Juliet*
7. Biscuits
8. To give a presentation with a partner about a famous person
9. Fat Larry, a TV chef
10. Glittery, silvery fairies
11. She helps out at the Infants after-school club
12. Mrs Cambridge
13. Mrs Vomit Bagley
14. *A Christmas Carol*
15. Tracy has to clean the whole Home

So you think you know about . . . family in Jacqueline Wilson's books? (page 80)

1. Vita and Maxie
2. Gran's
3. Australia
4. Andy
5. Mulberry Cottage
6. Her dad
7. None
8. Their pearl wedding anniversary
9. He's a taxi driver
10. Callum
11. McVitie
12. Elsa
13. Three
14. Because she's covered in tattoos
15. Her dad, Michael

So you think you know about . . . clothes in Jacqueline Wilson's books? (page 114)

1. White knickers and a hand-knitted cardigan, both with rabbits on them
2. A yellow frilly dress
3. A sparkly green suit, so she can dress up as Fat Larry
4. A black dress decorated with moons and stars
5. Blue-and-green striped polo shirts
6. A white-and-gold outfit
7. Designer jeans
8. Her Miss Kitty nightie
9. That she's wearing amazing clothes instead of school uniform
10. Her police hat
11. A safety helmet
12. A designer T-shirt and combat pants
13. A party dress with teddies on it
14. A sparkly T-shirt and trousers

Goodbye! (page 26)

1. Double Act
2 The Dare Game
3. Candyfloss
4. Jacky Daydream
5. Best Friends

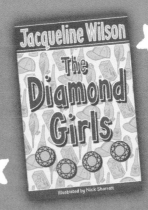

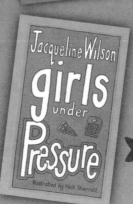